"*Reality TV* is a great template for any academic
—**KEVIN BRIGHT**, Executive Producer of *Frien*
Emerson College LA

"The author shares firsthand knowledge of beneficial and critical information regarding this ever-evolving segment of the industry. His reputation as a
genre leader is clearly well-earned." —**SEAN RANKINE**, Executive Producer of
Basketball Wives and *Basketball Wives LA*

"This is the *one* book you must use. Troy has done a fantastic job of organizing and presenting the material so that it flows beautifully, giving you a very
thorough road map to follow if you want to pursue a career in reality TV or just
want a better understanding of the form." —**GARRY HART**, Past President
of Paramount Network Television and current Chair and Professor of the
Department of Cinema and Television Arts, CSU Fullerton

"There is no one on this planet who understands better than Troy DeVolld the
medium and business of unscripted television. He is the Aristotle of reality
TV… and this is his "Poetics." —**CHAD GERVICH**, Writer/Producer: *Cupcake
Wars, Wipeout, After Lately, Dog With a Blog, Sex Sent Me to the ER*; Author:
Small Screen, Big Picture; How To Manage Your Agent

"The rock-solid yet amusing insights gleaned from Troy's book gave us just
the leg up we needed when pitching to and communicating with Hollywood
network execs and production companies." —**RONE BARTON AND LOU
AGRESTA**, Show Creators

"Troy DeVolld literally wrote the book on structuring reality TV."
—**JOKE AND BIAGIO**, Joke Productions / *ProducingUnscripted.com*

"This gem of a book gives you an inside glimpse of this genre that we've all
become so enamored of. Troy is a master in giving you the story behind the
story." —**JEN GRISANTI**, Story/Career Consultant at Jen Grisanti Consultancy
Inc., Writing Instructor at NBC, author of the books–*Change Your Story, Change
Your Life, Story Line*, and *TV Writing Tool Kit*

"Now in its second edition, *Reality TV* is chock-full of new and up-to-date
material that will arm you with the knowledge necessary to succeed. I recommend it to those wanting to enter the fray of reality programming or
for those wanting to cross over from narrative to this unique form of storytelling." —**RONA EDWARDS**, Film/TV Producer; Author of *I Liked It, Didn't
Love It: Screenplay Development from the Inside Out* and *The Complete
Filmmakers Guide to Film Festivals*

"This whole thing about reality television to me is really indicative of America saying we're not satisfied just watching television, we want to star in our own TV shows. We want you to discover us and put us in your own TV show and we want television to be about us finally . . . "

—STEVEN SPIELBERG in interview with *Rolling Stone*, April 26, 2007

AN INSIDER'S GUIDE TO TV'S HOTTEST MARKET

realitytv

2ND EDITION

TROY DeVOLLD

Foreword by Allison Grodner, Executive Producer of *Big Brother*

MICHAEL WIESE PRODUCTIONS

Published by Michael Wiese Productions
12400 Ventura Blvd. #1111
Studio City, CA 91604
(818) 379-8799, (818) 986-3408 (FAX)
mw@mwp.com
www.mwp.com

Cover design by MWP
Interior design by William Morosi and Debbie Berne
Copyediting by Gary Sunshine
Printed by McNaughton & Gunn

Manufactured in the United States of America

Library of Congress Cataloging-in-Publication Data

DeVolld, Troy.
Reality TV : an insider's guide to TV's hottest market / Troy DeVolld.
Description: 2nd edition. | Studio City, CA : Michael Wiese Productions,
  2016. | Includes bibliographical references.
LCCN 2015043175 | ISBN 9781615932436
LCSH: Reality television programs--History and criticism.
LCC PN1992.8.R43 D48 2016 | DDC 791.45/6--dc23
LC record available at http://lccn.loc.gov/2015043175

Printed on Recycled Stock

Contents

Acknowledgments

This second edition of *Reality TV: An Insider's Guide to Television's Hottest Market*, as with its predecessor, would not exist were it not for the generosity of a number of people and companies.

First and foremost are the many friends, coworkers, and others laboring in reality television, from whom I have learned so much and made so many friends and so few enemies over dozens of projects. Thank you. It's been a pleasure, even on the worst days.

Then there's Michael Wiese and Ken Lee, who believed, as I did, that media students and readers out there really do want — and need — to know more about reality television. I also extend my thanks to my dear friend and *The Sound Effects Bible / The Location Sound Bible* author Ric Viers, who put my idea for this book forward to them more than half a decade ago.

Thanks are also due to:

My parents, Robert and Gail DeVolld, who never faltered in their support of a son that they put through not only art school, but film school. There should be medals awarded for that kind of parenting.

Allison Grodner, who was kind enough to take on the foreword for this second edition and remains of my favorite Producers in the industry.

Patric Verrone, for contributing such a thoughtful foreword to the first edition and for his many years of championing for and rallying the reality TV community during his tenure as President of the WGAW and beyond.

My agent, Beth Bohn, who should charge extra for therapy.

Daniel Lawrence Abrams, for both his friendship and permission to share his Producers Guild of America panel's insights into the sizzle reel process in Chapter Eight.

The unbelievable Allee Willis, who continues to inspire me by her creative example and her litmus test for all good work: "Does It Have Soul?"

Derek Christopher, whose events have introduced me to interested students and aspiring reality professionals all over the world.[1]

Patricia Harrison, whose fresh eyes and support during the writing of the first edition were invaluable.

In closing, I'd like to offer my appreciation to the professionals who offered advice and quotes over the course of this book or who are otherwise cited within[2]: Eric Anderson, Paula Aranda, Avi Armoza, Michael Carroll, Christo Garcia, Chad Gervich, Mark Ciegelski, Adam Daroff, Nick Emmerson, Joke Fincioen, Albert Fisher, David Garfinkle, Brian Gibson, Dana Gould, Prof. Henry Jenkins, Anna Klassen, Thomas Lennon, Nancy C. Lutkehaus, Pam Malouf, Margaret Mead, Biagio Messina, Heather J. Miller, Les Moonves, Dan O'Shannon, Ken Paulson, Eduardo Penna, Hector Ramirez, Phil Rosenthal, George Schlatter, Steven Spielberg, Kevin Thomas, David Timoner, and John Wells.

---

1 If you want to book me for seminars, master classes, or anything else, drop a line to realitytvtroy@gmail.com and I'll put you in touch.

2 The author acknowledges the copyright owners of printed or otherwise recorded materials referenced in this book for purposes of commentary, criticism, and scholarship under the fair use doctrine. No specific endorsement of this book by the individuals cited should be implied.

How to Use This Book

I've lectured, moderated, or participated on many reality TV panels for learning institutions and professional organizations. The diversity of folks I've met at these events dictates that this book must appeal to an audience as broad as that of reality TV itself — a no-nonsense, no-filler guide helpful to both the interested television viewer and to media students and scholars. Further, I wanted to ensure that this book presented itself as a resource for the already-working story professional interested in exploring reality TV.

For reality fans, the second edition of *Reality TV: An Insider's Guide to TV's Hottest Market* provides a behind-the-scenes breakdown of their favorite shows, clarifying what is "real," and to that point, what "real" even means. How is raw footage produced and processed into compelling, must-see television? If I've done my job, *Reality TV* should demystify the process for you.

For film and television students contemplating careers in reality TV — a genre that accounts for more than half of all programs currently on-air in the United States[1] —*Reality TV* delineates the mechanics of reality TV from preproduction through post and provides real-world advice on topics like landing your first job and moving up the ladder once you're in the door.

Educators will, hopefully, find *Reality TV* vital to maintaining a current and relevant television and film curriculum.[2] Additionally, the book provides lesson plan–ready exercises (many new to this second edition) to hammer home the points made in each chapter.

Finally, working writers and producers in scripted film and television can use *Reality TV* as a primer before exploring their options on the reality/nonfiction side of the entertainment industry. Many previously

---

1 Partially owing to the ever-widening umbrella of what's referred to as "reality TV."

2 If you're not talking about reality/nonfiction in your curriculum, you're closing a rather large employment door to your graduates. Please consider it.

employed drama and comedy writers are fighting their way into the bizarro-world of reality TV. This book is a lifesaving guide to avoiding the political and professional pitfalls to which traditional scripted writers are particularly susceptible as they face the often counterintuitive "reality" of reality television.

However you plan to use this book, I hope you'll enjoy it and be able to put my knowledge and experience to work for you. And since no book can answer all questions, I look forward to hearing from you personally at realitytvtroy@gmail.com or through my blog, *www.realitytvbook.com*[3].

---

3 My only ask — please don't pitch me, and try to be as specific as you can with questions. I do limited consulting based on availability if you have more in-depth needs.

FOREWORD
BY ALLISON GRODNER

Even with its proven mass appeal and the fact that unscripted shows are in the majority on cable networks, there is still the sense that reality television creators are not quite equal to their scripted peers — just watch the Emmys! But the truth is, whether you are producing reality, scripted, or documentary television, the mission is the same: to tell a good story. You may start out with a script, an outline, or just a camera waiting for the unexpected to unfold, but in the end, we are all storytellers seeking to inspire, provoke, touch, and ultimately entertain.

I started producing unscripted television when it was just called television, but it definitely wasn't the path I intended to take. After graduating film school in the midst of a major writers' strike, I suddenly found that everyone I had worked for — pulling cable, setting up craft service, working for free (also called an internship) — was suddenly unable to hire me. The only person I knew who was still working was the award-winning documentary producer Arnold Shapiro. After only two weeks of unemployment, I found myself swept up into the world of nonfiction television doing shows like *How to Stop the One You Love from Drinking and Doing Drugs* (catchy title) and *Fatal Passions*. Eventually, I was lucky enough to be part of the original team that launched the hit CBS show *Rescue 911*, and from there I never looked back. The reality genre proved to be creative, limitless, surprising, daring, and sometimes, it could even save lives.

I am fortunate to be a part of one of those rare success stories as an Executive Producer for one of the longest-running reality shows, *Big Brother*. The fact that the show is still on the air is definitely a testament to people's continuing fascination with reality TV. There is also something to be said for the live, unexpected nature of the format as well as the explosion of new technology that keeps people watching three shows a week all summer long. Digital and social media technology have evolved and grown over our fifteen years on network television, and today you can stream all the live action directly to your phone or iPad with ease, providing yet another way to watch and interact with the show. This also means the day-to-day production is being monitored by hundreds of thousands of armchair producers — a blessing and a curse that ultimately keeps our story team on their toes.

This is an exciting time for storytellers across multiple genres and platforms and that includes unscripted. As technology expands exponentially, so does the demand for entertainment in new and exciting forms. We now have opportunities to produce reality shows for screens big, small, and virtual, and in ways never before thought possible.

Even with limitless possibilities, it is important to understand that just having a good idea is not enough. You must know how to produce and execute your idea.

That is where my friend and colleague Troy DeVolld comes in. With his vast and varied experience working on some of the most successful shows in this genre, he has used the pages before you to take the mystery and hopefully some of the "stink" out of what goes on behind the scenes of reality television. There is actually a lot of hard work, creativity, and, believe it or not, integrity that goes into producing unscripted television, and Troy does a great job of making that clear as well as laying out a great foundation for those just getting started in the business.

To those who are just graduating college, to those who are paying their dues in internships, and to all of the talented people who have helped shape this genre, there is and will always be a need and a hunger for content. It is our responsibility as established and aspiring reality producers alike to continue to raise the bar and find new and innovative ways to tell our stories. We should look outside the traditional reality tropes and gimmicks and strive to break the stereotypes of our genre, and stop trying to make noise just to make noise, working hard to make great, well-executed shows for the audience without losing the element of surprise and authenticity that makes unscripted work.

Allison Grodner has been a major player in the unscripted television scene since producing and directing the long-running series *Rescue 911* on CBS. Well-known as the creator and Executive Producer of the US version of *Big Brother*, Grodner's long list of credits includes *Plain Jane, Virtually in Love, You're Cut Off, She's Got the Look, Big Rich Texas, The Big Tip, Summer Camp, OMG! EMT, Brat Camp, The Family, Blow Out, Situation: Comedy, Family Business, Flipped,* the Emmy-Award winning docuseries *The Teen Files,* and the critically acclaimed HBO documentary *Small Town Ecstasy.* Grodner is a founding partner at Fly On The Wall Entertainment.

Introduction
Reflections on *Reality TV* and How the Second Edition Became Essential

W elcome to the second edition of this book on writing and producing reality television. Please don't look directly into the camera or acknowledge that I'm actually standing right here, as it's vital to the illusion of reality and the appearance of total spontaneity. Thanks.

Friends, relatives, and cynical media students love to ask me if reality shows are "real." Even on the most convoluted of series with the most cartoonishly contrived setups, I can tell them with a straight face that, at a bare minimum, the *reactions* are usually real — something scripted dramas and comedies will never be able to give the viewer. We, the home audience, will forgive the outlandishness of almost any premise in the name of witnessing real emotion on screen, so long as the content we're watching isn't riddled with obvious gaps in logic.

The mysteries of reality television are shrouded by the intentional obscuring of its production process from the public. As an unfortunate side effect, few who are interested in a career in reality have ever gotten the straight dope on where to start or what happens once you're inside the machine.

Why won't anyone just fess up and tell you how the shows are executed or how to get a job writing and/or producing them? It's almost as if the folks pulling the strings feel that the discovery of what goes into making reality shows would, like knowing the contents of the meat pies in *Sweeney Todd*, rob viewers of their taste for them.

So far, it hasn't. Reality continues to be a booming business, and the expanding content delivery landscape promises even more opportunities. Thankfully, many more media students and aspiring creators are taking it seriously.

While traditionally scripted feature and television screenwriting still carries a certain allure — it's unquestionably a sexier career than sorting out disagreements among Kardashians and assorted mob/basketball/baseball/football wives, tricking out somebody's old car, or watching a bunch of people compete to lose weight — many more people are taking an interest in the process than I'd expected back when the first edition of this book was published in 2011.

Plenty of shows have come and gone since the publication of the first edition. The controversial and wildly successful *Jersey Shore* was retired from the air in 2012. The refreshingly goofy *King of the Nerds*, one of my favorites, was cancelled in 2015 after just three seasons. But that's all micro-focus stuff. There are bigger changes to be noted than just a few landmark shows setting off into the sunset.

On the business side, major media companies ramped up an impressive spending spree, continuing to buy up independent production companies at an alarming rate, often at many times their EBITDA[1], compounding the fortunes of those companies' founders. Just check out some of the headlines that have run since the last edition of this book hit shelves:

ITV Acquires 80% Stake of New York–Based Leftfield Entertainment for $360m

FremantleMedia Pays $50m for a 75% Stake in SallyAnn Salsano's 495 Productions

UK-Based Company Buys $40m Stake in Gurney Productions

You might find it interesting to know that Leftfield was formed in 2013 (through the acquisition of Sirens Media, founded in 2005), 495

---

1   EBITDA: Net income with taxes, depreciation, and amortization added back to it. Most of these companies are being sold at many times their actual value as a revenue stream or for the values of the contracts they hold.

Productions was founded in 2006, and Gurney Productions set up shop in 2005.

Yes, these multimillion-dollar deals were all made for companies about the same age as your average fourth grader. The point I hope to make here, however, is that the people behind those deals all had to start somewhere, working for someone else and learning the craft. The tenacious SallyAnn Salsano and I are alums of Mike Fleiss's Next Entertainment, where we both worked on Season 6 of *The Bachelor* — she as a Supervising Story Producer, a notch above me as a Story Producer. Before starting his company, Scott Gurney was a Producer on PaxTV's *Cold Turkey* in 2004. Rebecca Toth, half of the founding partnership of Sirens Media, was an Associate Producer on Mandalay Media Arts' *Sahara* just five years before cofounding her company.

"Get Real, Get In, Maybe Even Get Rich" isn't just a catchy tagline for the back of this book, it's a declaration of possibility. The important thing to remember, however, is that most of the people who make the real money started, just like you, at a point where they were filling in time cards at someone else's company. They didn't all break into the business by selling shows or starting a company straight out of college. That's why this book is almost completely devoted to the storytelling and producing end of reality television, without spending *too* much time on the difficult process of creating and selling original content. As I always say, trying to break in as a show creator in reality is like trying to join the Army as a four-star general.

Get real. Get in. Maybe even get rich.[2] But remember — the first step to winning any game is understanding the way it's played.

Good luck!

---

2 Or, just make a good living. Nothing wrong with that, right?

Supervising Producer Heather Miller arranges scenework to create an episode outline. (photo by the author)

Story Is Story, and Story Is Written. Sort Of.

I'm not about to try to convince you that every word and action in a reality show is scripted. It's just not. Ever. Even the most heavily "produced" shows have *some* naturally occurring elements.

The recipe for every reality show is different. Sometimes writing and content manipulation are applied as sparingly as one would sprinkle a strong spice, and other times they're the main ingredients. Some shows follow a natural timeline and endeavor to play reality straight, in which case the story team's focus is applied to the compression of time. Other programs shred content like a salad shooter, stitching together bits of dialogue and action, repurposing scenes left and right.[1]

There is no reality show I'm aware of that's comprised of a straight-up, uncut piece of source footage. Someone's there, pulling strings behind the scenes to at least some extent, on every reality show there's ever been, compressing time and performing myriad other duties to make the end product more engaging and entertaining.

Why do we hesitate, then, to acknowledge the work of storytellers in the reality genre? If real life doesn't happen in

---

1 "Conjecture and aberration!" as one of my Editor friends summarizes the process, usually at the top of his lungs when something isn't working in the edit bay.

thirty- and sixty-minute increments complete with ad breaks, how can there *not* be some kind of creative work going on behind the scenes?

No mystery there . . . reality shows have writers and producers (all with unusual job titles) that shape story to bring you the most authentic end product they can — a passable imitation of life.[2]

But how does it all come together? On the facing page is a simple exercise that'll help you to understand the basics:

Amazing how all the action across all those episodes falls into pretty much the same order over the same number of acts every time, isn't it? How fortuitous that every week something *naturally* goes horribly awry with a budget or deadline not once but *twice*, the second time always worse than the first! Well, gang, if every fix or remodel was that problematic, pretty soon no one on Earth would let those shows' contractors and hosts anywhere near their gutted, mold-ridden, run-down fixer-uppers. I know I wouldn't.

In all fairness, a few things are bound to go a little haywire anytime you're doing a project with unskilled labor. But as to whether or not an entire project could be jeopardized by someone's wife leaving a hammer outside in the rain, well, our friends in the story department[3] are just the ones to blame for putting more than a little spin on that action.

How much spin?

Just look at how interview and voice over drive the story along. Most of the heavy lifting in home improvement shows is done with those devices — voice over and interview. Sure, a little gab throughout helps you to interpret actions that might be confusing without a little explanation, but moreover, it's that interview content and host copy that tells you *how you should feel* about what you're looking at.

For example . . . you've got a shot of a guy looking at a section of rotted flooring. Think about how much differently you'd react to hearing the host deliver each of these lines in conjunction with the image:

- "Ted sees this as a challenge. He'll have to replace the entire floor, and he can't wait to dig in with his new tools."

---

2 *Imitation of Life* was the working title of this book until reality writer Eduardo Penna jokingly asked me if such a pretentious title would be sold with a free wheel of brie cheese attached. *Touché,* Mister Penna. *Touché.*

3 Story Producers, Story Editors, and their support staff.

THE HOME IMPROVEMENT SHOW EXERCISE[1]

In high school, you may have peeked inside a frog or two in biology class. Ages ago, frogs became a standard tool for basic anatomical study due to the fact that their physiology makes them easier to dissect than most other types of animals. More pointedly, our little green friends have the misfortune of being comprised of easily identifiable guts.

In the world of reality television, basic cable home-improvement shows are my first choice as "lab frogs" because most of them share a similar construction and aren't generally too complicated. They easily demonstrate concepts like compression of time, use of host voice over and interview content to enhance stakes,[2] and that sort of thing.

Try this little exercise at home: Select any do-it-yourself home-improvement reality program and prepare to study two or three episodes. Make it easy on yourself and try a thirty-minute program first.

Grab a stopwatch and a notepad, settle in, and start viewing. Count the number of acts and jot down when certain events occur within the overall structure of the show.

During your review, keep an eye peeled for these specific moments:

- "Tonight On" tease (a glimpse ahead at the show you're about to see)
- Opening Title Sequence
- Introduction of the Host and Designer/Contractor
- Introduction of the Location, Homeowner, and Project
- Consultation
- Commencement of Work
- Introduction of First Hurdle to the Project[3]
- Overcoming of the First Hurdle
- Introduction of Second (Larger) Hurdle to the Project[4]
- Overcoming of the Second Hurdle
- Completion of Project
- Review of Project

---

1   When I set out to write this second edition, I wanted to write all-new exercises just to shake things up — but this one, to me, is so straightforward that it would be like trying to improve on the spoon.

2   "Stakes" is a term generally used to define what's at risk for participants of a program. No stakes, no drama. No drama, no show.

3   This probably happens just before an act break.

4   This also probably happens just before an act break.

- "Termite damage means the cost of the project could triple. It's the beginning of the end for Ted's dream project."
- "The good news is, the termite damage is confined to a small area. Ted's lucked out this time."

Wait a minute . . . you mean you could be looking at something that happened naturally, but was narratively tailored to suit the broader storyline?

Eeyup.

Like I said . . . story is story, and story is written. Sort of.

So Why Don't I See Writers Credited on Reality Shows?

Good question.[4]

Some networks and producers like to pretend that their shows aren't manipulated or scripted, not even a smidge, because they think it'll spoil the illusion. Others obscure the process as part of an ongoing effort to stave off unionization in their corner of the industry, a battle that's raged on for years.

One of the reasons it's hard to figure out who does what in reality TV is the fact that nonunion reality shops don't have universal guidelines in place to adhere to in defining writing and producing titles or responsibilities. The credit roll at the end of a show means nothing to the untrained observer who might be hunting for a "writer" credit, and what the heck do all those other weird titles mean?

While I've always preferred to take variations on the "Story Producer" credit to the alternate "Story Editor" credit, they're exactly the same gig nine times out of ten. On some programs, especially in the case of live shows with some produced-to-tape elements incorporated into the broadcast, story folks are even called "Segment Producers."

In the odd case where you do see the title of "Writer" fly through the credits, it most often represents the person who authors the host's on-camera patter and off-camera voice over . . . and even then, writing that host copy doesn't ensure the credit. I've written thousands of lines of voice over and host content for shows and have yet to be afforded a "Writer" credit. Not that I'm complaining, mind you. It's just that if a

---

4 Remind me to thank myself for asking it.

"Written by" or "Writer" credit is important to you on some spiritual or ego-gratifying level, you'd be better off concentrating your energies on sitcoms and dramas.

According to a 2007 independent study conducted by Goodwin Simon Victoria Research at the request of the Writers Guild of America West, the average Story Producer in reality television earned $2,000 to $2,500 per week[5] [6] compared to the WGA minimum rates of $3,600 – $3,800 per week commanded by lower-end sitcom staff writers. Figure in the pension and health benefits afforded to WGA members by mandatory contributions from signatory production companies and the pay chasm widens even further.[7] I don't even want to discuss the residuals[8] that reality folks never see, because then I'll start crying and you'll have paid for a very short book that didn't tell you very much.[9]

What Does a Story Producer Do, Exactly?

It's been said that Ginger Rogers could do everything Fred Astaire did, but backward and in heels. That's exactly what Story Producers and their companion Editors do in comparison to their traditional comedy and drama counterparts. Instead of the writers' room gang-scripting process employed by sitcom and drama scribes who furiously write and rewrite their material and that of their peers prior to and sometimes even during shooting, we're often bound by the limitations of content returning from the field, performing much of our work well into the postproduction process using only limited source material.

Yeah, I know. It's complicated. You should have seen my face when it was first explained to me.

One of my earliest reality mentors, *Fear's* supervising Story Producer Kevin Thomas, used to tell me that reality television was just like traditional writing, except you had to tell your stories with refrigerator magnets. To clarify, if you've ever played with one of those refrigerator magnet poetry sets, you know that you have an extremely restricted vocabulary to draw

---

5 http://www.wga.org/uploadedfiles/news_and_events/press_release/harsh_reality.pdf

6 Anecdotally, those pay rates have remained near that level for the last decade.

7 Don't give up yet! The good news is that employment in traditionally scripted television is seasonal, but reality production continues year round. I often do as many as three shows in a year.

8 Residuals are payments for reuse of work when shows re-air over and over again.

9 I've seen work I did near the start of my career repeating on cable as recently as the day before writing this chapter.

from. In reality television, you have a finite amount of source material[10] to tinker with once you return from the field and an awful lot of options to choose from when it comes to shuffling it into a story.

With fridge magnet poetry, there are millions of ways to arrange those tiny white words into coherent sentences — but in the end, you can't write a story about a buffalo if you don't have the word "buffalo" handy and you sure as heck can't put that buffalo on roller skates if the words "roller skates" aren't there either. Same deal with reality TV — if something didn't get shot, it doesn't exist. It's possible to completely fabricate scenes from odds and ends when it's called for, but it takes a lot of skill and extra effort to pull off.

While your dimwitted uncle Barry can spend twenty minutes coming up with the three-word magnetic poetry arrangement "two fingers tall" and be pleased with himself, your hipster roommate can take the same daunting wad of fragmented English and create a brilliant and moving haiku summarizing the human condition. Again, reality's the same way. It takes a while to develop your skill set, but once you know your way around the genre, your work can only get better.

In summation, good story producing is about finding the most effective ways to translate and arrange fragments of source material into a solid, engaging story.[11] You're going to have to bend a whole lot of time and space to get there, though.

Timeline? What Timeline?

Earlier, I referred to the compression of time as part of the Story Producer's job. Let's take a deeper look, using a theoretical calendar day in the life of an imaginary reality show subject, "Fred."

In the first episode of his series, Fred wakes up to discover that he's going to be evicted from his apartment if he can't find a job. Luckily, there's a message on his machine that says his dream employer has reviewed his resume and wants him to come in for an interview. Fred puts on a shirt. He gets in his car and goes to the interview. His interview goes well. He goes out to lunch with friends and worries aloud about what will happen to him if he doesn't get the job. At the end of the lunch, he gets a call telling him that he landed the job he's been dreaming about. His

---

10 Videotaped content in its rough form, as shot.

11 Which is not to say there aren't a few dimwitted Uncle Barrys working in reality TV.

friends cheer! That night, Fred takes his friends out for a drink. His apartment and life are saved!

This would have been quite a day for Fred, except that the events above took place over three weeks, and were carefully assembled to get the viewer to buy into the illusion of it being a single, action-packed day. And that voice on the answering machine? Well, since Fred got the message late at night and then erased it, we had to record facsimile audio on a handheld microphone in the edit bay using a production assistant we thought had a nice voice, which we then put a "telephone" effect on and added over a pickup B-roll shot of Fred's answering machine.[12]

Scenes and elements (interviews, dialogue, interactions between characters) don't always occur in the order you see in the final product. For all you know as a viewer, material that looks like a single day in someone's life (like Fred's above) could be culled from a month or more of shooting and edited to create wall-to-wall drama. Scenes and fragments A, B, and C could have taken place anytime, anywhere, and as for what you're hearing people *say*, well, that's a whole different can of worms. Statements can be handily sliced, diced, and reordered to say almost anything in a process we call "frankenbyting."[13]

Authenticity

No matter how much content gets swapped around, trimmed, or re-edited, the end result must comply with the one overarching, undeniable rule of reality television: *The integrity and perceived authenticity of story cannot be compromised.* Audiences are savvier than you think, and will turn on you if they feel they're being outright bamboozled.

Leave too many seams showing in a hard-scrambled Frankenstein's Monster of a show and audience trust evaporates like a shallow puddle on a July afternoon. True, only 30% of viewers surveyed claim that it matters to them that the content of reality shows is real,[14] but I dare say that the other 70% won't long tolerate a show that doesn't at least strive to make it appear so.

---

12 If you ever call a reality producer on this kind of manipulation, you'll likely get a phony baloney reaction similar to that of Captain Renault in *Casablanca* during the raid on the back room at Rick's Café Americain: "I am shocked, *shocked*, to find gambling going on in this establishment!"

13 The process of editing individual words or phrases within sentences together to simulate a new thought or statement. Some companies try hard to avoid these.

14 2005 Associated Press / *TV Guide* poll.

Back to the big metaphor here — just as you notice that a fridge magnet sentence like "Jane to the mall bought pants" is grammatically incorrect (thereby calling attention to itself), missing story points or unconvincing fabrications blow the illusion of reality by breaking the flow of information perceived to be authentic. Sure, you get what the shows are going for, just as you understand the fractured language of "Jane to the mall bought pants," but because the viewing experience is compromised, you don't buy the idea that what you're seeing is real. The suspension of disbelief necessary for viewers to immerse and invest themselves in other types of TV shows still applies to reality.

The following are a handful of examples of the kind of shoddy story work that can leave viewers scratching their heads:

- Two characters haven't been getting along for most of an episode, and now they're in a scene together laughing it up like old friends. What happened? When did they resolve their differences?
- Three characters are having a conversation in the middle of the day. A response edited into the action clearly shows that it's dark outside, compromising the perceived continuity of action.
- A character is speaking in interview, but his words are sliced and diced to say something else — and you can hear every wild change in pitch during the "frankenbite."

Like a pimple on the nose of a prom queen, even the smallest glitch creates a massive distraction from the whole picture. Distraction leads to disengagement, and disengagement leads to disaster.

So how do you keep an audience from detecting any lapses in authenticity once you start noodling around and shuffling your material to maximize content? By minding your continuity and following the rules of good storytelling.

Continuity and Story Basics

Remember: if it looks or sounds fishy to you, it's going to look and sound fishy to the viewer. Continuity, defined by Wikipedia as "consistency of the characteristics of persons, plot, objects, places, and events seen by the reader or viewer," is of the utmost importance.

As a result, in order to *really* work for viewers, a reality show must be laid out with the same care and craftsmanship that any other form of screen storytelling demands, complete with well-defined characters and story arcs, turning points, and gratifying resolutions.

Break out your favorite screenplay books and read them again and again. Go read *Save the Cat!* or anything else you've wanted to pull off the Film/TV shelf at your favorite bookstore but haven't invested in. Watch a good traditionally scripted movie or TV show and think about what makes it work for you as a viewer. Watch a lousy one and ask yourself why it *doesn't* work for you.

It's okay. This book will be here when you get back.

You back already? Great. I presume you're now chock-full of knowledge and a deep, abiding desire to serve story and con-

> "Continuity is really a mixed bag. I try to address anything that seems blazing obvious to me. Sometimes you have to cheat an angle or cut around something to make it work. Sometimes the Editor and I are privy to a thing or two that we just don't point out to anyone else. Sometimes we play kind of a 'Where's Waldo' game to see who can spot the continuity gaffe."
>
> **—HEATHER J. MILLER**, Co-Executive Producer, *Booze Traveler*

tinuity above all else. Just in case you're one of those impatient types who didn't actually run off and read anything else on story first, let me just lay out some basic rules for you:

First, *the premise alone is not the show.* You can have the most brilliantly conceived show ever made, but it'll die on its feet if you populate the show with shallow, interchangeable participants or fail to explore your characters. Why? Because engaging characters in reality television have backstories, opinions, and motivations for their actions. This is why it's important that your cast has meaningful conversations and exchanges, or at the very least punctuates their actions with thoughtful interview content. You must be aware of what's at risk for them *personally*, what the "stakes" are, to invest in them. If Player X wants to win $100,000, what differentiates him from anyone else on the show? If he needs that money to buy a bigger house for his expanding family or in order to take care of his ailing father, we can identify with and invest emotionally in his win. Character motivation makes the stakes, and it's crucial that you compel your audience to care.

Second, *stories in reality television arc just as stories in movies or other television shows do.* A happens, B happens, C happens. Set up a problem, build stakes, resolve. Every action must have a consequence, whether realized immediately or later in the episode or series overall. Each episode has its own problems to deal with and escalates the stakes surrounding the season's bigger issues on the way to the season finale where everything must be somehow resolved. If you're just "cutting for noise," a mistake novices often make in which big-energy scenes (like arguments) become more important than character development or a calculated ramping up of story, you'll bore your audience silly. Your viewers want to follow a story, not just have their eyeballs and earholes assaulted for half an hour, an hour, or even two hours.

The more you know about story, the more you know about story. Period. I don't care if you're writing movies or comic books or reality television shows, the basics always apply. Now, I don't aim to give you the idea that reality television writing and producing doesn't present its own unique set of challenges . . . putting good stories together from bits and scraps is one of the toughest and least understood jobs in the entertainment industry, and just as most novice screenwriters read a lot of scripts and see plenty of movies before setting out on their journey, so should anyone wanting to tell stories in the reality genre get hip to the formats and devices that have been successful in the past.

Which brings us to . . .

A Brief History of Reality Television

B efore we dive into the particulars of how reality shows are written, it's good to know a bit about how they came to be in the first place.

Let's be clear — this is by no means a complete history of reality television, as that would easily make for its own book. But here's an overview to help you get an idea of how the genre evolved into a staple of our television diet.

Origins and Pioneers

Long ago and far away, in a galaxy broadcast in black-and-white, dinosaurs like the Milton Berleasaurus and the mighty Ed Sullivanadactyl ruled the airwaves.

Texaco Star Theater, *The Ed Sullivan Show*, and even the venerable *CBS Evening News* made their debuts between May and August of 1948, but one curiosity among that pack of summer shows really stood out. Allen Funt's *Candid Camera* featured the jovial Funt playing hidden-camera gags on unsuspecting marks, working them into a befuddled lather before finally letting them off the hook with his signature phrase, "Smile, you're on Candid Camera." The adaptation of *Candid Microphone*, Funt's radio show, to television successfully added a new dimension to the formerly audio-only hijinks while giving the world what may have been its first "reality" program.

Yes, reality TV may well have started with a prank show. Even in the late 1940s, you weren't safe from getting *Punk'd*.[1]

While media scholars generally agree that *Candid Camera* was the first reality show, one could certainly argue by today's all-encompassing definition of "reality" that Ted Mack's *The Original Amateur Hour*, a talent-search program, may actually own the title. It had premiered on the DuMont network months before on January 18 of the same year.[2]

No matter who got there first, the ball was rolling by the end of the summer of 1948. Networks caught on that viewers loved being able to see themselves, if only vicariously, on television. Whether they felt represented by the everyman conned into participating in one of Funt's crazy schemes or by a gifted nobody in search of fame and fortune on *The Original Amateur Hour*, people tuned in in droves. Reality was off to the races, and the next quarter-century would produce long-running titles like *This Is Your Life*, *Wild Kingdom*, and the BBC's *Come Dancing*, whose premise laid the groundwork for the global phenomenon *Dancing with the Stars*.

> "These early days of 'reality' television were innocent, truly human, and lacked the hard edge and back-stabbing elements so prevalent in today's programs. It was a softer and gentler era and one that deserves its own place in television history. I am proud to have been a part of it."
>
> —ALBERT FISHER, President/CEO of Fisher Television Productions Inc.

In 1973, twenty-five years after the premieres of *Candid Camera* and *The Original Amateur Hour*, *An American Family* brought to PBS the true-life trials and tribulations of the Loud family, sewn together from seven months of documentary-style coverage shot in 1971. The twelve-episode series pulled few punches, even as parents Bill and Pat Loud separated and filed for divorce while their son Lance made history as one of the first openly gay characters ever featured on television.[3]

The show was a bona fide phenomenon, airing to an audience of some ten million viewers and landing the Louds on the cover of *Newsweek*. American cultural anthropologist Margaret Mead wrote in *TV Guide* that

---

1 *Punk'd*, which ran on MTV from 2003 to 2007, is but one of many contemporary examples of the revisited *Candid Camera* format.

2 Interesting sidenote: Albert Fisher, quoted in this chapter, holds the remarkable distinction of having produced for both *Candid Camera* and *The Original Amateur Hour*.

3 An interesting sidenote: Lance Loud had been a resident of the Chelsea Hotel, the residents of which were featured in Warhol's groundbreaking *Chelsea Girls* five years earlier.

An American Family's reality format was "as new and significant as the invention of the drama or the novel — a new way in which people can learn to look at life, by seeing the real life of others interpreted by the camera."[4]

Reality television continued to proliferate over the next decade and a half with segment shows like *Real People* dropping in on ordinary people with extraordinary stories . . . like Captain Sticky, a flamboyant self-styled hero who championed consumer rights, and Ron "Typewriter" Mingo, the world's fastest typist. In a 2004 interview, creator George Schlatter stated, "We would do the research, and we would show up, and whatever happened, that was what was going to happen, you know?"[5]

While reality had certainly proven its popularity, there was nothing to prepare viewers or the entertainment industry itself for the boom triggered by the 1988 Writers' Guild of America strike, arguably ground zero for the explosion of reality television that still reverberates today.

At the time of the strike, reality shows were the networks' only option for getting fresh content on the air, generating demand for shows like John Langley and Malcolm Barbour's gritty and long-running *COPS*, which made its debut in 1989. What could be more thrilling and less expensive to shoot than following cops and crooks around with a camera?

> *"The Original Amateur Hour* was hosted by Ted Mack and was about as true to 'reality television' as you could get. Amateur performers (singers, dancers, musicians, novelty acts, comics, etc.) would perform before a live audience. Home viewers would cast their votes via telephone and/or postcard for their favorites. Winners would come back and try to become a three-time champion and go on to the finals held annually at New York's Madison Square Garden. "Graduates" from this classic series included Frank Sinatra, Robert Klein, Pat Boone, Ann-Margret, Gladys Knight, and even the Reverend Louis Farrakhan."
>
> —**ALBERT FISHER**, President/CEO of Fisher Television Productions Inc.

While *COPS* stormed the turf of traditionally scripted drama, *America's Funniest Home Videos* made a comic splash when it blasted into living rooms the same year on the ABC network.

---

4 *TV Guide* quote referenced in *Margaret Mead: The Making of an American Icon* by Nancy C. Lutkehaus.

5 April 20, 2004 interview by Ken Paulson on *Speaking Freely.*

Audiences went nuts for the new wave of reality programming even as the networks began to fall hard for the cheap fix reality shows provided them. Even the biggest reality shows of the late '80s and early '90s cost a fraction of what nets had spent on star-driven sitcoms and dramas. Reality show participants could be wrangled at a cost barely north of a baked potato and a handshake at a time when major stars could cost producers $60,000, $70,000, even $100,000 an episode.

When Mary-Ellis Bunim and Jonathan Murray premiered their strangers-in-a-house reality series *The Real World* on MTV in 1992, they credited *An American Family* as their inspiration. *The Real World*, whose inaugural season filled a nine-story New York co-op apartment with young strangers, was a breakout smash. The opening narrative for the show spelled out its thesis: "This is the true story . . . of eight strangers . . . picked to live in a house . . . work together and have their lives taped . . . to find out what happens . . . when people stop being polite . . . and start getting real . . . *The Real World*."

Concerns that the show could not be brought back for a second season due to the likelihood of retaining a cast of non-actors were met with an ingenious response from producers Mary-Ellis Bunim and Jonathan Murray: A new cast in a new location each subsequent year would ensure that the drama would always remain fresh.

The Real World's second season, set in Los Angeles, was arguably an even bigger hit with audiences, and by season three, when a San Francisco home was populated with cast members like the irrepressible bike messenger punk Puck and HIV-positive activist Pedro Zamora, the show truly hit its stride as the new gold standard for youth-oriented reality programming.

By 2000, the big broadcast networks, rapidly losing market share to basic cable, were milking new cash cows like *Survivor* and *The Amazing Race,* shows that far outperformed much of their scripted competition while simultaneously relieving some of the financial strain the nets were feeling.

Contemporary Reality

Reality television marches on, with scores of new titles cropping up every year. Scholars and critics are coming to grips with the fact that the medium isn't about to fade away and is now worthy of critical discussion rather than simple dismissal. So pervasive is reality television in today's broadcast universe that in 2003, Les Moonves, President of the CBS Network, informed the *New York Times* that "The world as we knew it is over." He should know — he's the executive who opened the door to Mark Burnett and *Survivor*.

Criticisms of the Genre

Aside from the legions of justifiably peeved comedy and drama writers displaced by reality content's encroachment onto their turf, many critics deride reality TV as mind-numbing junk. In many cases, I agree with them — but I also believe that it's wrong to assume that it's all garbage.

What I find so amusing about the critics who compulsively tilt at reality like Don Quixote to a windmill is the dual standard by which they judge reality against other genres.

Some of them complain about reality's almost uniformly beautiful cast members while simultaneously giving a pass to the gorgeous casts of shows like *Friends* or *Gossip Girl*. Others moan about the genre's unbelievable situations and setups . . . you

> "What you're watching is an amateur production of nothing."
>
> — **DANA GOULD**, Comedian[1]
>
> ---
>
> 1 From a 2010 appearance on Showtime's *The Green Room with Paul Provenza*.

know, because a bunch of celebrities hosting a backyard talent show on *The Surreal Life* is so much more far-fetched than that *Star Trek* episode where the USS *Enterprise* finds itself awash in self-replicating, faceless, purring throw-pillows called "tribbles."

Many critics also feel sure that the numskulls who turn up to participate in reality shows are somehow affecting viewers' own behavior with their immoral, anything-for-fame antics. It's perfectly acceptable to those same critics, however, for a scripted show to present a sympathetic serial killer like *Dexter,* a sex-addled writer like David Duchovny's character in *Californication,* or a crystal-meth-selling high school science teacher as played to perfection by Bryan Cranston on *Breaking Bad*. Again, though, the moment a booze-fueled date with single hottie Tila Tequila heats up on *A Shot at Love,* it's the end of the civilized world.

To that sort of criticism, scholar Henry Jenkins, while Director of Contemporary Media Studies at MIT, commented, "Don't look at the characters on reality TV, look at the audience usage of those characters.

Contemptible behavior, even if successful, is still condemned by an increasingly participatory audience."[6]

Another common belief among critics is that the success of reality television depends on the lowest common denominator of viewers tuning in. Not so. Witness the success of cable's Bravo network, home to *Flipping Out*, *The Real Housewives of New York*, and *Vanderpump Rules* among other hits. Bravo's sponsors have flocked to the network for years to access their statistically affluent, educated audience . . . an audience that just happens to love reality shows.

Product placement and integration[7] in reality also raises the ire of critics. Over the years, shows like *The Apprentice* have served up challenges that incorporate sponsors like Domino's Pizza even as pizza-adverse contestants on *The Biggest Loser* chomp away at Subway sandwiches and Extra sugar-free gum. Product overload can be seriously distracting, but is it really any more distracting than seeing these products written into favorite traditionally scripted shows? In 2007, sitcom creator Phil Rosenthal (*Everybody Loves Raymond*) testified before the Telecommunications Subcommittee of the House Commerce Committee (on behalf of the Writers Guild of America West and the Screen Actors Guild) regarding the pervasiveness of product integration and its impact on story. Phil hilariously summarized, by screening a string of clips, a storyline on the scripted series *Seventh Heaven* in which characters relentlessly plugged Oreos right up to the moment one character proposed to another by presenting his beloved with a wedding ring — a wedding ring concealed *inside an Oreo cookie*.

For all reality's faults, I still liken critics who blanketly bash it while favoring sitcoms and dramas to wine snobs who can't just enjoy an orange soda now and then. Good reality rivals the best traditionally scripted television for entertainment value, and its positive impact on popular culture can be felt just as deeply, if not more so, than its negative.

Okay, I can sense that I'm going to have to sell you on that one.

Consider the number of people emboldened by shows like *The Biggest Loser* to make positive changes in their lives. The popular series

---

6 Excerpted from transcripts of the October 2005 MIT panel discussion "Is Popular Culture Good for You?"

7 "Placement" is when you see a name-brand soda on the table. "Integration" is when the name-brand soda's not only on the table, it's also part of the storyline.

for NBC started a national movement to get in shape that echoed across America, making heroes (and moguls) of personal trainers Bob Harper and Jillian Michaels. While the show has been taken to task by critics for its wall-to-wall product placement, one can hardly argue that any other show in recent history has done so much measurable good for viewers.

Also worthy of note is reality television's lead role in broadening minority representation on television. Reality shows typically sample a far larger ethnic base than scripted television; one need go no further than shows like *Big Brother* or, again, *The Biggest Loser* to support that claim. One of my favorite shows in recent years is *RuPaul's Drag Race,* in which a number of hopefuls compete to become the next drag superstar in a brilliantly innovative competition presided over by legendary drag performer RuPaul. A show of this kind couldn't have existed on television mere decades before when LGBT performers were simply told that "gays have no place on television"[8] and Lance Loud was considered an on-screen anomaly.

While criticism of reality television continues to trend toward the negative, my take on the stacks of lousy reviews it generates is this: Well-executed story with engaging characters and surprising turns should be offered immunity to preconceived prejudices against a genre that's already spent its entire life being lambasted as a critical "less than."

Sure, a lot of what's on is downright distasteful, poorly executed, and dimwitted, but can't you say the same thing about gross-out, male-driven sitcoms and ripped-from-the-headlines past-their-prime legal shows?

Come on, critics, start playing fair.

---

8 Noted actor Charles Nelson Reilly recounted just such an early network experience in his one-man show, *Save It for the Stage,* later memorialized in the doc film *The Life of Reilly.*

Chapter One Exercises

EVOLUTION OF CONCEPT EXERCISE

Just as *Candid Camera* begat shows like *Punk'd*, *Boiling Point*, and *Scare Tactics*, choose another landmark reality show and name at least three other shows that built on the concept.[9]

In each case, make note of the twist on the concept that came before it. For example, *Punk'd* played elaborate pranks on celebrities, *Boiling Point* rewarded the most patient prank target with a prize, and *Scare Tactics* sought to frighten the subjects of its pranks.

CRITICISM EXERCISE

Ask three friends to describe a reality show they love or despise. Ask them why they feel strongly about the show either way. Ask them the same question with regard to a favorite scripted program. Do you find a bias in favor of or against reality programming?

SUGGESTED READING ON REALITY CRITICISM

Reality Bites Back: The Troubling Truth About Guilty Pleasure TV by Jennifer Pozner.

---

9 If you're stuck for ideas, try *The Osbournes* and *The Surreal Life*.

The Seven (or Seventy, or Seven Hundred) Kinds of Reality Shows

We live now in what I like to call "The Age of Lists." Every week, there's a new countdown show detailing the top ten celebrity meltdowns, a magazine article giving you the top fifty new stars to watch out for, or a blog entry recounting the last hundred things Nicolas Cage has had for breakfast.

Okay, I made the last one up. But mark my words, one day you'll be reading the Nicolas Cage breakfast blog and thinking, "That DeVolld guy was right on the money."

Point is, you probably want to see a list of the kinds of reality shows that are out there, but it isn't easy for me (or anyone) to nail them all down. Genres and subgenres are tough to categorize in this age of hybridized programming.

Let's say that, using traditionally scripted entertainment as an example, you lean toward comedies. You can page through your cable guide and find yourself a horror comedy, a romantic comedy, a sci-fi comedy, or a dramedy. They're all comedies, but they're something else, too.

Same deal with reality television, though if you had to put everything under major banners, this list might make for a good starting point:

- Documentary/Docuseries
- Reality-Competition: Elimination
- Makeover/Renovation
- Dating
- Hidden Camera / Surveillance / Amateur Content
- Supernatural
- Travel/Aspirational

Let's look at these one at a time.

Documentary / Docuseries

The documentary/docuseries category is probably the broadest of the mix. Whether you're getting a tour of Mariah Carey's pad on *Cribs* or watching police officers pull a suspect out from under a backyard kiddie pool on *COPS*, this is the umbrella that covers them both. Heck, it even covers most house-reality shows like *The Real World*.

So what differentiates the documentary from the docuseries? Well, while documentaries are one-offs, docuseries play out more like a traditionally scripted soap opera, following action over a series arc.

There's been a great deal of controversy surrounding some of the more successful docuseries as to just how "real" their content may be. In recent years, MTV's *Laguna Beach* and its spin-off, *The Hills*, followed the lives of a gaggle of young, good-looking (if seemingly dense) characters, drawing fire from critics and fans alike over scenework that often read as poor long-form improvisation hung on a rickety framework. You can't shoot perfectly framed, beautifully lit material on the fly forever . . . so if a docusoap looks too good to be true, it just might be.[1]

The Hills is a prime example. One of the show's stars, Lauren Conrad, spilled the beans in a June 2009 guest appearance on the ABC talk show *The View* when she responded to a question about a phone call seen on the show with the statement: "To be perfectly honest, I wasn't on the other line of that call. That was filmed and I wasn't on the other end . . . So I didn't even know about it."[2]

---

1 In its 2010 series finale, *The Hills* ended with a crane shot reveal of a cast member standing in front of a backdrop on a studio lot as it was being wheeled away. Depending on your interpretation, this was either a nod to the show's staginess or a far-out joke at the expense of those who claim the show was scripted.

2 *The View* ©American Broadcasting Company.

While I'll make no ruling here on the authenticity of *Laguna Beach* or *The Hills*, it should be noted that when working in the docusoap format, your every misstep in story producing and editing registers tenfold in comparison to other reality programs. Clumsy docusoap work, to seasoned reality fans, yields a viewing experience akin to riding a rocket-powered church pew down a potholed road, every bump unbelievably jarring.

I'd also lump under this banner most of the "social experiment" shows, where groups of people are brought together for the primary purpose of seeing them react in an environment, immune from challenges or elimination. Says veteran Producer David Garfinkle, "Human nature is fascinating [. . .]. These types of shows are all about human nature — the good, the bad, and the ugly — and it's fascinating to watch."[3]

It's also worth nothing that there has been a boom in recent years in family and occupational docusoaps and docuseries, featuring unusual families and groups of people who share an occupation. Whether it's the trials and tribulations of the Roloff family on *Little People, Big World* or a group of shipmates crab-fishing in dangerous waters on *Deadliest Catch*, this recent trend has boomed in popularity since the early 2000s.

Reality-Competition / Elimination

The gladiators of ancient Rome have been replaced in modern entertainment by bug-eating backstabbers vying to keep themselves from being voted off an island. At least that's the simplistic impression a Martian might get from watching reality-competition shows.

All reality-competition programs feature some sort of prize and the hopefuls vying to claim it, whether that prize is honor, cash, a unique opportunity, or all three. Their exploits can span full seasons as with *Survivor, American Idol*, or *Dancing with the Stars* just as easily as they can be completely self-contained on individual episodes as with shows like Thom Beers' *Monster Garage*, where each episode challenged a team of builders to complete an unusual project in a specified time frame.

Reality-competition participants can compete directly against either each other or, very often, a more abstract antagonist like time itself . . . like when an individual or team must beat the clock in order to win.

---

3 Kimberly Nordyke, "Why TV Networks Are Buzzing Over Social Experiments," *The Hollywood Reporter*, June 3, 2014.

The elimination mechanisms are always clearly established on these programs, as you can't arbitrarily drop participants and viewers will tune out quickly if they can't follow the logic behind who stays and who gets sent home.

The trick is in ensuring that the suspense lasts right up to the last moment . . . if one player suffers a major setback, you can't telegraph that they're the only one likely to be eliminated or viewers will skip the end of the episode. This is why you so often find that extra round where two or three cast members are singled out for possible elimination before some-one's head finally rolls.

The classic *Survivor* has its own brilliant failsafe built in, as players compete in each episode first for immunity, then in an elimination round where all participants cast ballots to see who will next be "voted off the island." You have to watch all the way to the end, as nothing can be taken for granted until the final vote.

There are many elements of the docuseries at play in reality-competi-tion shows, notably the idea of players living together in a confined space (a home, a campsite, etc.) and interacting on a human level between chal-lenges, deepening your investment in the success or failure of participants you feel that you've come to know by allowing you to see them as people in addition to players.

Makeover/Renovation

Whether the subject is a face or a place and whether the tools of choice are scalpels, makeup kits, or box shrubs, makeover and renovation shows are all about one thing: transformation.

Popular examples of this kind of reality show include *Extreme Home Makeover*, in which deserving recipients have their dilapidated homes renovated into tailor-made showplaces, and *Queer Eye for the Straight Guy*, a long-running show that rescued dumpy subjects by revamping their wardrobe, look, and living spaces with the help of a small army of hip, cultured gay advisers.

Wilder examples include *Extreme Makeover* (not to be confused with *Extreme Home Makeover*), a 2002 show in which participants were given complex makeovers including plastic surgery and extensive dental work. To see how easily the lines between makeover/renovation and reality-com-petition can be blurred, one need look no further than *The Swan*, which made its debut in 2004. The ultra-controversial Fox series took a group of women with low self-esteem, granted them plastic surgery and dental makeovers as with ABC's *Extreme Makeover,* but then had them compete against one another in a beauty pageant.

Other crossovers into the Reality-Competition universe have included *House Rules* for TBS, in which three married couples renovated different areas of three project homes each week in a bid to win the deed to the property they'd been assigned to.

Dating

No-brainer here. Boy meets girl, boy meets boy, girl meets girl, and drama revolves around whether they hit it off or not. Examples of this type of program include *The Dating Game*, *Blind Date*, and *Love Connection*.

Reality-competition hybridizations most notably include Mike Fleiss's ABC juggernauts *The Bachelor* and *The Bachelorette*, which present a single man or woman the opportunity to select a mate from some two dozen hopefuls looking for love — complete with the now-infamous "rose ceremonies" that eliminate ladies and fellas along the way. While the prize is only love (and sometimes one heckuva ring), it's probably the most successful dating / reality-competition hybrid in American television history.

The popular Japanese series *Ainori*, which lasted an astonishing four hundred episodes, even had an element of travel built in as romantic hopefuls traversed the globe in a pink bus, trying to hook up with each other without getting the boot by pledging their love and then having it go unrequited.

Hidden Camera / Surveillance / Amateur Content

Likely the oldest strain of reality on television, what started with *Candid Camera* has evolved into shows like *Punk'd*, *The Jamie Kennedy Experiment*, and *Scare Tactics*. The goal is always the same — capture natural reactions from unwitting participants placed in unusual situations.

Lumped in with hidden camera programs are clip shows that rely heavily on surveillance or amateur bystander video for material. *The Smoking Gun: World's Dumbest Criminals,* and *When Animals Attack* are good examples.

As with all other genres, there's always a great reality-competition hybrid example. The best of the best in this category is *America's*

Funniest Home Videos. With more than twenty seasons completed since its 1990 debut (1989 if you want to count the one-hour special that birthed the series), this monster hit for ABC invites viewers to submit funny home videos for a chance to win substantial cash prizes. With spin-offs around the globe, the biggest cash prize probably belongs to the show's affable Executive Producer, Vin DiBona, who had the good sense to import and tweak the already-successful format from Japan.

While there is often a hidden camera feel behind shows in the supernatural genre (which we're about to get to), I wouldn't lump them in under this heading.

Supernatural

While most often represented by investigative things-that-go-bump-in-the-night shows like *Ghost Hunters* or *Paranormal State,* supernatural shows may also feature anything from cryptozoology (the study of unclassified beasties like Bigfoot and the Loch Ness Monster) to psychics.

Most supernatural reality shows can be traced back to MTV's *Fear,* which to my thinking always owed a debt to the film *The Blair Witch Project* for its aesthetic — shaky handheld cameras and plenty of fixed night-vision stashcams.[4]

The magnificent *In Search Of . . . ,* which ran from 1976 to 1982, often documented subjects as diverse as Bigfoot and UFOs, though its frequent focus on mysterious historical figures (the disappearance of Amelia Earhart, for example) might call its classification as a purely supernatural series into question. Me, I grant it a pass for mystery.

Travel/Aspirational

With the average American's work schedule, television shows are as close as some of us will ever get to spending weeks at a time in exotic destinations halfway around the world. Most of us probably won't find ourselves driving Aston Martins or spending thousands of dollars on bejeweled handbags either. For us housebound types with anemic checkbooks, there will always be travel/aspirational shows to let us experience the globe-trotting good life, if only vicariously.

---

4   A remotely operated camera providing high, wide coverage; in some instances, a hidden stationary camera.

The terms "travel" and "aspirational" aren't always married . . . for every *Lifestyles of the Rich and Famous* or *How'd You Get So Rich*, there's a show like *Rick Steves' Europe* or Huell Hauser's *California's Gold*, where your host goes sightseeing without dropping too much loot along the way.

Well, there's your list. At least, *my* list. Happy now?

Chapter Two Exercise

Just to hit the point home about the evolving nature of reality programming, check your current listings and find an example of each of
the following: documentary/docuseries, reality-competition, makeover/
renovation, dating, hidden camera/surveillance / amateur content,
supernatural, and travel/aspirational.

Now, review the list. Are any of the shows you selected hybrids?

Bonus: Can you name any shows that might defy classification
using the examples provided?

The Reality of Reality

When a professional colleague of mine found out I was writing the first edition of this book back in 2010, I told him that I'd be covering the basics of writing for reality television . . . how stories are told, what the workflow is within a production, and so on. He responded with a laugh and told me that if I ever found out what the workflow was *supposed* to look like on a reality show, I should let him know.

The logic behind the jab was simple. Reality shows are such a jumble of overlapping responsibilities and nonstandardized titles that trying to explain definitively what one job or another entails is virtually impossible. Also, as hard it is to wrap your head around, reality show workflow is as malleable as clay when it comes to the creative side of things.

Let me explain.

On a traditionally scripted comedy or drama, it's easy to identify who the writers are, who the showrunners are, and what everyone's roles are within the production. As the various job duties in scripted television are so well defined by guilds and unions and years of doing things the same way, it's easy to delineate where one job ends and another begins.

Not so with the reality television workplace. Story Producers are alternately titled as Story Editors or Segment Producers, their involvement beginning in preproduction . . .

or production . . . or postproduction. I've worked on shows where Story Producers shoot their own material in the field, shows where they're not involved until post, and while I've never worked on one like it, I know of shows where Editors are required to go it alone in sussing out story from oceans of source content, assuming the full weight of the storytelling responsibilities themselves.

Confused yet? The reality of reality is it's like the Wild West, and as a result, few shows are ever run exactly alike.

That said, let me give you a quick walkthrough of one of the constants — the chain of command in any production, starting at the top.

Overview: Production Hierarchy

While it takes an awful lot of people to put a show together, these are the folks you'll find yourself dealing with most often in the story department. I apologize in advance for the head-scratching that the fluidity of these titles may induce.

The **NETWORK:** Whether they're across the lot, across town, or across the country, these are the folks who must ultimately sign off on everything. Even your production company reports to them since the network is footing the bill. In addition to network execs (who now often take Executive Producer credits just like those at your company), you'll also find lawyers and S&P (standards and practices) folks who'll pore over your content to make sure there's nothing there that's indecent or likely to get them sued.

The **EXECUTIVE PRODUCER:** Now here's a confusing credit. The Executive Producer may or may not be the show's creator, and could just as likely be a talent who's negotiated the credit as part of their package. In still another scenario, an EP could be a network exec or the owners of the production company you work for. The only ones you'll be concerning yourself with are those directly empowered to oversee your work and give you notes, whether they're the owners who sign your checks or the network gang.

The **CO-EXECUTIVE PRODUCER:** Sometimes the Co-Executive Producer is a show's creator, sometimes it's a valued member of the production company's team who's negotiated the credit. I've often seen it afforded to someone who'd otherwise be titled as a Supervising Producer (see below).

The **LINE PRODUCER:** While your only interaction with the Line Producer may well be negotiating salary or ensuring that your time cards are processed, this individual is also charged with keeping the show running at or below budget.

The **SUPERVISING PRODUCER:** The Supervising Producer credit is usually applied to the person or persons who run your show on a day-to-day basis through all three stages of production. You may find some Supervising Producers titled as Co-Executive Producer, though not all Co-Executive Producers are Supervising Producers. Supervising Producers report to the Executive Producer, ranking just below the EP in most cases. Supervising Producers are responsible for the overall production to the limit that the Executive Producer delegates control.

The **SENIOR STORY PRODUCER** (sometimes **SUPERVISING STORY PRODUCER):** The Senior Story Producer credit can be negotiated even if the person in the position doesn't actually supervise anyone, but in an ideal environment, the Senior Story Producer oversees a team of Story Producers in order to preserve continuity of tone and story throughout each season of a show. In the absence of a bona fide Senior Story Producer or Supervising Story Producer, an Executive Producer or Co-Executive Producer may assume these duties.

The **STORY PRODUCER**: The Story Producer's job varies slightly from project to project, but typically consists of (at the very least) composing story outlines and compressing source material for time and content into a coherent story. One of the stranger things about the Senior Story Producer and Story Producer positions is that they may commence work at any point from preproduction to post, depending on how a project is organized.

The **FIELD PRODUCER:** These are the folks on the front lines of production. They may function alone or, when Story Producers are brought on during preproduction or production, as part of the larger story team. Wise Story Producers will allow the Field Producers to act as the liaison between the story department and the production itself, preserving an often necessary (and certainly recommended) buffer between story and talent. Some Field Producers are simply titled as Producers.

The **ASSOCIATE PRODUCER** or **CO-PRODUCER:** Typically the lowest-ranking producers, these folks often take care of specific tasks delegated to them by producers above them in the hierarchy.

The **ASSISTANT STORY EDITOR or STORY ASSIST:** This helpful character exists to help you organize materials and execute story function.

They search transcripts and logs for elements needed to tell the story, sometimes working with Loggers and Transcribers to locate and compile content.

The **LOGGERS** and **TRANSCRIBERS:** These folks review and summarize source material in order to make things easier for you to find later. While some production companies' in-house Loggers do handle transcription, most production companies will send interview content of any length to a transcription house for review due to the time-consuming nature of executing word-for-word breakdowns of interview tapes. Good work from these people can really free up a lot of your time on complex productions.

Now that you know the people you'll be dealing with in story, the next chapter will fill you in on when everyone jumps onto the train. First, however, a few words of caution before you board.

Plotting a Career from Day One

Understanding the hierarchy I've just described is critical.

While I'll be reserving most of my commentary on your career for Chapter Seven: Get to Work!, here's something you should know about the hierarchy within reality television: Learn what you love *early*. Every job you take binds you more heavily to a career track that can, down the line, become difficult to deviate from. For example, I can count on one hand the number of people I've seen leap from story producing to editing and vice versa.

If your plan is to ultimately become an Executive Producer, you'll find that the industry has a definite bias favoring producers who work in the field (on set) versus working in post.

As you read this book and consider your first steps toward a career in reality, really think about what you'd like your career to look like.

Chapter Three Exercises

THE IMDB EXERCISE

Choose an Executive or Co-Executive Producer from the credits of a hit reality show. Look up their name at *www.IMDb.com* and see what positions they've held on different shows over the years.[1]

While not all IMDb profiles are complete, you'll get a great overview of what a career looks like. Titles may shift up or down,[2] and you'll also notice that many of the most respected working EPs spent years working their way up to running a show.

THE "LONELY AT THE TOP" ALTERNATE IMDB EXERCISE

While shows often have a great many Executive Producers listed, remember that many of those EP titles are negotiated by network execs, the talent's management, and the stars themselves on occasion.

Look at the number of Story Producers on a major show and compare to the number of Executive and Co-Executive Producers. While the numbers may seem close, search the Executive Producer and Co-Executive Producer names online. How many of the EPs are at network level or are talent / talent management?

---

1 For EPs at network, you can check for articles announcing their job moves at *www.Variety.com*.

2 My own career is a great example of title shifting. The important thing to me is to just keep working, and sometimes that means taking a lesser title / lower-rung gig once in a while if it means a chance to have fun on a show that interests me.

The author takes notes while watching the first season of a reality series, in preparation to take on season two. Once a series is in motion, learning to emulate the existing style is key; unless, of course, there are specific directives to move the show in a different direction. (photo by the author)

Preproduction

Preproduction, the time in which planning gets done prior to going into production, is an iffy stage for Story Producers, who may or may not be involved at that point.

Personally, the most rewarding shows for me are the ones where you're participating from the onset instead of relying on your Executive Producers, network folks, and Field Producers to somehow cook up terrific setups that will eventually translate into a tight show with all the pieces you need, making all your "refrigerator magnets" available.

Even if you're one of the lucky Story Producers who works with a show from start to finish, much has already been accomplished by the time of your arrival in the preproduction process.

By the time you walk in the door, your casting department and Producers have already selected the show's participants and "cast for conflict," ensuring that your cast members won't be happy get-along campers. One classic example of casting for conflict was the signing of Ron Jeremy and Tammy Faye Messner for season two of *The Surreal Life*, a VH1 series whose premise was built on filling a Los Angeles home with oddball celebrities to see how they'd get along. The pairing of Jeremy, an adult film star, and Messner, a career Christian minister and televangelist, became one of

> "The balance of the workload between Field Producers and Story Producers is crucial to the creative process of making a good show happen and make sense. The Field Producer needs to know how to shoot for the edit; meaning it is important to understand how things will be cut into the show. I think it's so important to know how to manage your time well in the field and know when you've got the right sound bites, scene openers and endings, and B-roll. You've got such limited time and money to make things work that you constantly have to trust that you are getting what the Story Producers need to cut a scene and make it work in the arc of the episode."
>
> —**MICHAEL CARROLL**, Producer

the most interesting in the entire run of the series. Why? Because there was no way the two could coexist under one roof without being at odds about *something*.

Of course, making the most of those kinds of pairings takes some engineering, which is a big part of your first step in the process.

Reviewing Past Episodes and Casting Materials

If you're working on a series that's already got a full season or two in the rearview mirror, spend your first day watching old episodes and getting a feel for what the production company and network expects. Unless you're asked, don't try to reinvent the wheel — just get to know what kind of final product everyone wants to see from you.

Additionally, if they're available, review casting materials including application forms and videotape for the final cast. If you're dealing with a celebrity cast or anyone with an Internet presence, check them out online. Get to know your characters and start thinking about where the potential for conflict lies, because without conflict, you've got no show.

Then, sit down with the people who are going to be making everything happen for you once the cameras start rolling (or, perhaps, just did) . . . your Producers and Field Producers.

Downloading with Your Producers

Just as you're probably going to check out a map or enter your destination into a GPS before a long trip, it's always good to know which way you're going before you hit the road when it comes to story.

If your show has Field Producers, they'll be hard at work organizing the shoot to come, as they play the major role in corralling and capturing story material for you on the front lines of production. They do the bulk of the story legwork on set, and will have (or have recently *had*, depending on when you come aboard) the most face time with the cast. If you've got a good team in place, you'll have little to do but take notes and offer a handful of suggestions once you're shooting. If you're *not* asked to be in the field, their take on how events went down will be invaluable in helping you sort out your story.

For now, though, ask them about the challenges and scenarios they're setting up and for any insight into the cast and planned activities that they can offer. They will have plenty to relate.

Sketching Out Your Profile Interviews

On or about the first day of shooting (and almost surely within the first week), time will be set aside to conduct "profile interviews." The purpose of the profile interview is to introduce your characters to the audience in a way that makes them instantly relatable and helps the viewer decide who to identify with and root for. As a rule, good interviews ask questions that can't be answered with a "yes" or "no" and push your subjects to answer thoughtfully in full, complete statements. As the interviewer's voice is seldom (if ever) heard in reality shows, responses that come in fragments like "yes" or "that's correct" do you no good as they can't stand alone in edit.

TIP Always remember, questions posed in an interview must be incorporated into the answer. If I ask you what your favorite band is, and you just say "U2," that statement cannot stand on its own if I cut away to it during a scene. However, if you incorporated my question into the response, saying "My favorite band is U2," it would make sense as a complete thought.

Now let's imagine we've got two contestants whom we need to set up in wildly different ways to make conflict pop if and when (hopefully) it happens. How can we get the most mileage out of their profile interviews?

Frank is a surfer on the comeback after an injury. In reviewing his tapes, you find him to be all smiles, gregarious, and likable.

On the other hand, there's Penny. She's a sarcastic bigmouth in her interview tapes, her audition paperwork tells us she's very particular about where she surfs, and she can't stop name-dropping or talking about her moneyed family.

Prior to the interviews, make a list of what you feel are important questions to have answered. Beneath each question, imagine the perfect response in italics, always in the form of a statement. Why? Because being in front of the camera can be intimidating for some people, and if they need help coming up with an answer that fills your needs, you've got one right there for them.

TIP Don't ask generic questions in profile interviews. Do your homework and formulate questions that will yield emotional or revealing responses.

Remember, since profile packages are usually pretty short, your goal is to formulate interview questions that will help the viewer get a feel for the character as quickly as possible. You can ask as many questions as you have time set aside for, but be aware that only a handful will make it into the profile package at the top of the first episode!

Let's start with Frank's first five questions. After reading his application for the show and reviewing his audition tape, here are some questions designed to bring out his personality while conveying his real backstory:

FRANK

Please tell us your name, age, and where you're from.
My name is Frank, I'm twenty-five, and I was born in Maui.

How long have you been a surfer?
I have been surfing since I was four years old.

We heard that your dad had a lot to do with your interest in
surfing. Tell us.
*My dad was a surfer who won a lot of major tournaments, and I always
wanted to be like him.*

Tell us about your injury and how it has or hasn't affected your
surfing.
*I shattered my leg in four places in a car accident about six years ago.
They told me I'd never surf again, but here I am, better than ever.*

Your application says you have a strong desire to inspire people
by competing on this show. Tell us that, and why.
*I'm here because I want to inspire people. I think it's important to show
people that you can overcome anything that gets in your way.*

Don't you like Frank already? I know I do.

Now let's look at the first five questions we might ask Penny, who we need to establish as someone likely to be an antagonist to Frank:

PENNY

Please tell us your name, age, and where you're from.
*My name is Penny, I'm twenty-two, and I'm from Long Island, New
York.*

Your application says you come from a prominent family of hote-
liers. Tell us about your family's business and how it helped you
discover surfing.
*My family owns a small chain of hotels in exotic places, and grow-
ing up I had access to the greatest beaches in the world. That's how I
discovered surfing.*

You said on your application that you're entering this contest
because you want to be "the Paris Hilton of surfing." Tell us
that and explain why.
*I'm here to show the world rich girls can surf too. I want to be the Paris
Hilton of surfing because I think it's a niche that's waiting to be filled.*

You also said on your application that public beaches suck
because of "beach bums and college students." Explain.
*I never surf on public beaches because they're dirty and crowded and
frankly, I don't want to have to fight for waves with beach bums and
college students. Public beaches suck.*

Penny's personality sure comes across in just a few statements, doesn't it?

Once you have your profile interview questions worked out, pass them along to your Field Producer. They'll fold in several of their own before they set out.

Will you end up getting the answers you're hoping for? Maybe. I'll tell you more on how to make sure you do in the next chapter.

The Preliminary Outline

Once you and your Field Producers are on the same page, write up a single-sheet outline organizing the activities that will take place over the shoot dates for your episode. It's one thing to have a set of call sheets and objectives lined up, but having the full episode laid out is a big help in remembering that you're not just shooting a bunch of separate events and hoping a story unfolds — you're hunting specific story beats that will eventually come together into a meaningful story. Pleasant surprises along the way may provide for some great moments — but for now, keep the big picture in mind.

Here's what one of my outlines might look like.

"BEACHES" EPISODE 101

DAY ONE

Interviews

- Profile interviews

The Competitors Meet, Get Room Assignments

- Tara and Dana have history / bad blood, watch for conflict / establish rivalry in OTF

Flagler Beach Group Surf

- Winner receives a new board from show sponsor XYZ Boards
- All surfers OTF after their runs

Dinner, Bedtime

- Promote discussion of emerging friendships or frictions
- OTF as relevant

DAY TWO

Balance Challenge

- Surfers stand on row of small tiki heads on beach, last one to fall off wins immunity
- OTF as relevant

Local Outing: Flagler Beach Surf Museum

- Surfers find out winner of competition this season will have their own exhibit added
- OTF as relevant

Dinner, Bedtime

- OTF as needed, angle on having great/lousy time so far

DAY THREE

Breakfast

- Surprise! Elimination will be taking place in five minutes — chaos in the house

Elimination Ceremony

Fallout From Elimination Ceremony

- OTFs with all re: elimination

Now your story team in the field has their marching orders . . . these are the story beats you expect to see, barring any unforeseen circumstances.

Now that you've mapped everything out so fastidiously, you can just insert characters and wait for the story to happen just as you wrote it, right?

Not so fast. Just wait until production gets under way.

SPECIAL TIP / Preproduction for Live Shows with Taped Elements

While many reality shows have weeks or months of time set aside for production, some live-broadcast reality-competition programs will include brief segments of produced-to-tape material to air as part of their broadcast. These short packages (which can range from less than thirty seconds to as much as several minutes) must be turned around in a number of days, not weeks or months, so it's wise to plan out a detailed "shot list" and interview copy to ensure that you get all the stuff you need to make a great package. Again, the four- or five-day turnaround on these packages doesn't leave much room for error, so be sure your field team brings back the goods!

When composing your shot list, be sure to specify your B-roll needs as well. If you can't set up your location or make transitions from point to point visually, you're sunk. For example, if your cast travels to Nebraska, they can't just appear there. You'll need a bus, car, train, or plane shot, local B-roll, and establishing shots of the location they're going to . . . even shots of them entering the building.

Chapter Four Exercises

INTERVIEW PREP EXERCISE

Imagine that one of your favorite celebrities is about to be on a reality show. Write a ten-question profile interview that would summarize that celebrity's personality and career to someone who had no idea who he or she was, as well as set up his or her hero or villain status on the show.

In reviewing your questions, ask yourself if answering these questions authentically would produce the desired result or if the celebrity would be forced into playing a caricature of him- or herself. Are there any tweaks you'd like to make to ensure a better response?

OUTLINE EXERCISE #1

Imagine your family or another group of people that you know well have been cast in a reality docusoap about their lives.

Following a six-act structure, create an outline for a first episode based on upcoming events organic to their lives.

OUTLINE EXERCISE #2

Watch an existing hour-long docusoap, then re-create the outline in the format shown earlier in this chapter.

Once you've completed that task, create an outline for an episode that would immediately follow the one you just saw, moving the storyline forward and remaining true to the action already in play.

Do you find it easier or more difficult to build on story already in motion? Why?

Me, hard at work on an episode of a reality program. (photo by Lacy Augerlavoie)

A full season's worth of field notes. While time-consuming to write in the field, they save a lot of work in post. (photo by the author)

Production

As I've said earlier, Story Producers can be folded into the mix at any point along the timeline. If you're starting during the production phase, it's a lot like stepping out your front door and being whisked down the street by a parade. Production, the period during which your show is taped, features the complex dance in which Camera Operators, Sound Mixers, other Producers and curious network folks are all buzzing about thinking about everything but what you need in order to make the show happen.

In a well-controlled location, you will keep an eye and ear on the action from a remote area referred to as the "video village" or the more formal "control room," where monitors can relate what each Camera Operator and Audio Mixer is getting on set.

Why monitor the action remotely? Fewer bodies live on set means less scurrying out of the way when a Camera Operator is trying to follow a subject. Keeping the set relatively clear also allows your cast to settle in and not have to perform to a gaggle of strangers running around with headsets and whispering to each other on the edge of earshot.

Field Notes

Good field notes, which recount a shoot day's activities in a format that includes time of day and content, are essential to postproduction later.

If it's up to you to take your own field notes on set, don't let more than two or three minutes go by without making an entry. These notes are your road map for reviewing story content later, and the denser your notes, the less time you'll spend scanning through material in post. Before you start, be sure your watch or whatever timepiece you'll be referencing in your entries is in sync with the time being recorded by the cameras. Ballparking time can result in your notes being several minutes in either direction from the time code actually recorded, making postproduction content review a nightmare for you and your colleagues.

If you're on location during production, bring a laptop, but also bring a legal pad and pens in case anything goes screwy.[1] I've learned that power on location can be spotty and that even a solid charge on the best of batteries won't see you through a full day's shoot in most cases. As laptops go, I'm a large fan of the smaller netbooks, perfect for on-location note-taking and far less cumbersome than a full-size model. Investing in additional batteries is a great idea and well worth the money.

When taking your notes, keep each entry brief, as you'll be making them all day. Remember, too, to keep the language simple so that you can use your word processing program's search function to find keywords later. If you're really fond of something that you want to remember in post, add the all-caps word GOOD to the end of the entry. If you know something happened, but aren't sure whether it was well covered, add the word REVIEW so you'll know not to count on it until you review content down the road. Other words I frequently employ are FUNNY, FIGHT, and CRY. Three or four weeks from now, when you're sitting in your office a thousand miles from set and the source material isn't yet ready to review in the system for some reason, you can at least be reviewing these notes and working toward guesstimating scenework.

A three-minute sampling of notes from the field:

10:57	Frank is first to arrive at the house.
10:59	Zoe arrives. Funny exchange with Frank about her pink luggage. FUNNY, GOOD
11:00	Zoe trips on way to pick a bedroom, breaks lamp. FUNNY, REVIEW

---

1 Reliance on written notes alone is a mistake . . . you'll likely cramp up, or worse, be asked to type up your notes later.

If you're working a shoot with multiple cameras that are in different locations on set, take note of which camera or crew is covering the action you're seeing. While footage is often grouped for your Editors down the line (meaning they'll be able to see all camera content at the same time in their system), the setup you'll be working on for review and assembly of the material you'll be passing along may not be set up the same way. So, if your "A" and "B" camera crews are shooting the arrivals, but the "C" crew is in another location (let's say, in the car capturing reactions as people are being driven up to the house), you might want to make your entries like this:

10:57   Frank is first to arrive at the house. (A, B, C)

10:59   Zoe arrives. Funny exchange with Frank about her pink luggage. (A, B) FUNNY, GOOD

11:00   Zoe trips on way to pick a bedroom, breaks lamp. (A, B) FUNNY, REVIEW

You can't be everywhere at once . . . but taking great notes from wherever you happen to be will free you up to hunt down the stuff you *didn't* see for review later.

Hot Sheets

At the end of each day, a Story Producer or Field Producer is usually required to create a "hot sheet" detailing the highlights of the day in a one- or two-page summary that will be emailed to members of the production team and (sometimes) network execs after wrap or early the following day. These are used to track story and to keep others informed of major changes that may affect the action down the line.

The reason hot sheets must be executed and delivered so quickly is that if the field team gets even a day or two behind on them, the Producers away from set and back at the office are prevented from making any timely constructive input or helping to avoid chasing down content that they don't want or need for creative or legal reasons.

Another word of advice on hot sheets: be objective and never, ever, EVER[2] oversell action when summarizing the day's events. Why? Because getting people who weren't on set too excited about specific actions

---

2 I can't insert enough "evers" to make this point emphatically enough.

means they'll expect to see those moments in the show, even if the story takes different turns in post.

Here's the kind of hot sheet I like to see:

"BEACHES" HOT SHEET: DAY ONE (07/09)

SUMMARY

Arrivals at the beach house went smoothly with a few character-defining fun spots along the way: Zoe took a few tumbles throughout the day and there is much murmuring throughout the house about how she'll manage to ride a surfboard if she can't even walk. She and Frank became fast friends, becoming our only co-ed room share.

Tara and Dana are old rivals on the competitive circuit (established in interview and underscored by some great reaction shots) and did their best to avoid each other during the morning surf at Flagler Beach today.

To everyone's surprise, uptight Penny won the surf-off, winning a new longboard from XYZ Boards. Her gloating afterward caused some animosity.

Only one blowup today: Penny's declaration about public beaches and "surf bums" didn't sit well with the others during her post-challenge gloating. Frank called her on her poor attitude and disdain for the surfing lifestyle, and the rest of the gang piled on. As a result, Penny spent most of the day after lunch alone, and in midafternoon interviews stated that she is "already over these losers."

Generally, the gang is excited about tomorrow.

There's enough here to show that story is developing, but enough restraint in relaying the info that it reads in a straightforward and factual manner.

Here's the kind of hot sheet you don't want going around:

"BEACHES" HOT SHEET: DAY ONE (07/09)

SUMMARY

Arrivals at the beach house went smoothly today except it's totally obvious that Zoe is an uncoordinated fool who will probably drown herself if she ever gets near a surfboard.

Tara and Dana hate each other, and it shows. Expect big blowups there!

Bitchy Penny won the surf-off and a new longboard, and started a HUUUGE fight back at the house afterward when she went off about surf bums and Frank got mad at her about it. She is already an outcast — don't be surprised if she doesn't come out of her room again for the rest of the show.

Boy, do I hate hot sheets like this one. Everything is oversold, there's tons of conjecture about what will happen in the days to come, and character types have become so crystallized that if Penny wakes up tomorrow and apologizes, Tara and Dana get their heads in the game, or Zoe simply manages to not drown, it'll be a disappointment to everyone who expected something else to happen. Hot sheets like this one can jam up the note process in postproduction when your execs and the network start seeing rough cuts that don't deliver what the overly hyper, exclamation-pointed hot sheet content implied.

Interviews

Let's revisit the interview process for a moment now that we've moved on to production, as your characters are now in motion and your needs have changed.

The purpose of interview content gathered during production is two-fold: to provide clarification of action or emotion in anticipation of or in reaction to an event, or to provide context in establishing locations or purposes for being at those locations.

Using interview in any other way is usually superfluous to story. Why would a character simply narrate an action we can *clearly* see is happening?

Interviews Versus OTFs

Once things that demand commentary start going down in the field, you and your Field Producers have a decision to make: pull your cast aside for a small amount of time during or just after important events to grab a few quick OTF (On the Fly) quotes and responses, or hold off to do formal sit-down interviews every few days to recap events.

I'm a big fan of the OTF interview because the reactions are so much more authentic. You'll get tears, passion, laughter, rage . . . big, big energy. If you wait a few days to ask someone to recap an event in a more visually composed setting (I've worked on shows that rely only on formal interviews conducted several days, a week, even two weeks apart), you'll likely lose that sense of emotional immediacy — a high price to pay for a pretty interview shot.

In fairness, formal interviews have their own advantages. If you're crushed for time in the field, you can cover a lot more ground by getting many days' worth of content in one sitting. You have time to mull content over, figure out how you think it'll be used, and tailor your questions and desired responses more closely to what you'll be needing them for.

Here's another exercise for you that will illustrate the usefulness of formal interviews in comparison to OTFs:

Remember that analogy I made where I compared home improvement shows to lab frogs? Well, put on your lab jacket and goggles again, because I'm about to have you take that scalpel and t-pins to your favorite hour-long series.

Grab that same old pad and pen and cue up three episodes of your favorite show, preferably one where participants don't spend all their time in a uniform of some sort. Now watch the episodes, keeping track of what people are wearing in their formal interviews. It's easier if you pick one or two people rather than trying to track a full cast.

Be sure to watch for:

- Characters wearing the same outfit in interview over multiple episodes or seeming to change outfits during commentary on one scene. Indeed, almost anytime a cast member is wearing an outfit in interview that does not match what they are wearing in-scene, you're looking at a formal interview.
- Hairdos and haircuts that change over the course of interview clips within the same episode. Why? Because an interview done in April may contain content that can be used to make a point in June, if you get my drift.
- Content that addresses specific actions versus content that more generally addresses character relationships.

A little more about that last point: On viewing, you'll soon discover that ultra-generalized statements made in formal interviews are evergreen. An interview from the second day of shooting may provide just the right sentiment to end the series with, and most viewers don't think twice about what anyone's wearing in an interview, so anything said anytime, anywhere, can be applied to a scene to cover a difficult edit point or remind you of the presence of a character who hasn't got much to do in an episode.

No matter whether you opt for OTFs, formal interviews, or a mixture of both, here are a few things to remember:

Interview questions must be formulated in a way that helps to drive your story. Talk for talk's sake is deadly boring. *Say something* if you're going to pull the viewer out of action to listen to someone comment on it.

Last, but not least, make sure to nail the essentials when composing your questions and guiding your answers. You absolutely must cover these bases in order to survive post:

- Establish all locations. Example: "Where are you going tonight and why are you going?" *"Tonight, I'm taking Larry to a restaurant to see if he gets along with my friends."* Why? Because without these, there's no way to set up your location other than showing signs or describing the location in on-screen text . . . and even then, you won't be able to convey why your characters are there or what's expected to happen.

- Establish stakes (what's at risk). Example: "Do you like Larry and, if so, what would happen if tonight went badly?" *"I like Larry, but if he can't hang with my friends, I don't think I'll be able to go out with him."* Why? Because if we don't know what characters stand to gain or lose from an interaction, there's no reason to care about it.

- Pick up some content you can use to compress time. Example: "How long did Larry talk to your friends and how did it go?" *"Larry and my friends talked for about an hour, and I could tell they really liked him."* Why? Because it's awfully hard to compress time effectively without cutting away to interview, and the audience benefits from knowing what they should be taking away from the scene.

- Introduce any characters we don't know yet. Example: "Who is Jill and what kind of problem could she pose for Larry?" *"My one friend, Jill, has never liked anyone I've introduced her to. I've known her since college, and she can be hard to get along with."* Why? Because people want to know who they're watching and how they figure into the big picture.

- Document emotions or reactions that may not fully telegraph in-scene. Example: "You were smiling, but what was going on in your head?" *"Outside I was smiling at Larry, but inside I was getting angrier and angrier that my friends were being such jerks to him."*

Why? Because sometimes, viewers might not pick up on subtleties or what you might find to be brilliant subtext.

- Get summary statements to cap scenes. Example: "How did Larry do, and how will this affect you in the future?" *"Overall, I think Larry did well meeting my friends. They really grilled him, but he held his own. I think I'll go out with him again if he asks."* Why? Because when action alone doesn't tie things up, it's necessary to put a bow at the end of a scene to ensure that it registers as something worth recalling later in your storyline.[3]

Forecast Bites

Don't forget to go after what I call "forecast bites" that give us something to ponder in your characters' futures. Instead of just asking how cast members felt when x or y happened to them, ask them how they felt *and* how they think it will affect or bias them, their team, or another player for the rest of the time they're on the show. Instead of coming home with a simple "I thought what Penny did was uncalled for," you'll wind up with "I thought what Penny did was uncalled for, and I'm pretty sure none of us will ever trust her again." A bite like that sets up Penny as a possible villain for the rest of your show and gives her something to prove . . . maybe even teeing up an entire "B" story somewhere down the line about her either trying to regain the trust of the team or trying to manipulate them by using the fact that they think she's a liar now. These gems are perfect for ending scenes or episodes on a thought to be revisited later.

Remember, too, that it's okay to ask for specific pre-scripted statements in addition to responses to questions, as I mentioned earlier in the book. As talent sometimes reacts adversely to having words put in their mouths, though, always couch the ask by saying something like, "I really need this short statement to help me out in post. If you don't disagree with the statement, could you please say this phrase for me as written?"

Be sure to cover as many bases as you can, even if you're not sure you'll use specific answers or statements in post. It's always better to bring back more than you need than less. Remember: If your Field Producers are conducting interviews for you, they may not necessarily understand why you need everything you're asking for. It's critical that you maintain that

---

3 Word of advice: Try your best to start and end scenes on in-scene actions and statements whenever possible.

respectful, open line of communication with them, explaining why you're asking them to bring back specific content.

While it may seem to contradict my edict that you should cover all your bases, you should, at the same time, gun for concise answers. When an interview response trails for twenty, thirty, or forty-five seconds, you should allow the interviewee to finish, then ask them to recap the same thought in just a few sentences. While a lengthy response may sound authentic and conversational to you, you have no idea what an eternity thirty seconds is in the end product. In a half-hour show (presuming twenty-two minutes of content plus commercials), one thirty-second bite would be more than 2% of your total content run time.

> "Story Producers need interview bites that tie it all together and cover anything that might not have been caught on camera. Their job is tough because later in post, they only have the footage that the Field Producer has shot and given them to work with. If the Field Producer doesn't deliver on what's needed then it isn't happening ... period. There's no going back."
>
> — **MICHAEL CARROLL**, Producer

If you're pressed for time with your interviews (sometimes you don't have the luxury of spending forty-five minutes asking questions), train yourself to listen for breaks in your interviewee's responses. Ask yourself if fragments of their responses break as complete sentences, remembering also that Editors can usually pull out "ums" and "uhs" easily to tighten the replies.[4] A response like "Well, you know, Judy and I went down to the, um, uh, hot tub and Frank and some of the girls were down there talking about me, I wasn't sure what to think because, uh, being the first day and everything, I thought it was kind of early to be having opinions" could actually work out fine in post. We'll talk more about paring down interviews when we get to postproduction.

There are a number of camps when it comes to scripting interview content. Some subscribe to the "tell me what you're going to do, tell me what you're doing, tell me what you did" school of thought, which gives you the most complete range of source material to pull from later.

Why all three versions of this question? Because it'll give you the greatest number of options in post.

Let's say that your cast member is a surfer who makes his own boards, and you're interviewing him after he's given away a board to another cast

---

4 Most easily when words before or following end or begin, respectively, with sharp consonant sounds.

member whose own board was destroyed. The asks you'd make and statements you'd be chasing for later use are:

Let's say you've just seen Judy smash up her board. Tell me what happened and what you're about to do so she can stay in the competition.
Judy broke her board, but because she's come so far and worked so hard, I think I'm going to give her one of my custom longboards so she can stay in the competition.

Let's imagine that you're giving the board to Judy right now. Tell us what you're doing and why you're doing it.
I'm giving one of my custom longboards to Judy because I'd hate to see her have to drop out of this competition just because she has nothing to surf on this afternoon.

Let's imagine again that you've just given Judy the custom board. Tell us why you did it.
I gave one of my custom longboards to Judy. I would have hated for her to have to drop out of this competition just because she didn't have a board.

Advanced Interview Techniques

While we've already discussed interviews from the standpoint of knowing what kind of questions to ask and why, here are a few helpful tips on the more complex stuff — everything from composing the shot to dealing with problematic interview subjects.

Composing the Interview Shot

Every show should have a standardized format for interviews, and whether you're shooting in a special area or in front of a greenscreen so that your subject can be digitally placed in any environment, basic composition never really changes.

A subject should never be placed in the dead center of a frame, or the shot will appear stagnant and dull. Subjects should be placed either left of screen facing slightly to camera right or right of screen facing slightly camera left. It's sometimes helpful to set arbitrary guidelines to help mix up the visual style, as with male characters being positioned screen left facing right and female characters positioned screen right and facing left.

To establish an eyeline when conducting an interview, position yourself just slightly to the opposite side of camera from your subject's position and at lens height. Be sure you're at the same eye level as your subject, and be certain to brief them that they should be answering to *you* and not the camera. Be sure to stick close to the camera and that your subject's gaze crosses the lens to arrive at your eyes on the opposite side (in other words, if your subject is framed camera left, you should be on the right side of the camera).

While good interview content composition calls for that slightly off-center eyeline, there is one rare occasion when I think a subject's gaze should be directly into camera, and that's when they're calling out a castmate who's not in the room, saying something like "Watch your back, Jeff. I'm gonna get you." Use of this device, sparingly, will make such special content disarmingly impactful.

Checking Your Audio

While your crack Sound Mixer (or, at the very least, Camera Operator) should be paying attention to how things sound, be sure to keep an ear out for everything from dogs to airplanes to the clattering of heavy bracelets or other jewelry.

Train yourself to listen for these things that can wreck your content:

- Nearby chatter of cast and crew
- Audible music, however faint or far away
- Cell phone rings, even on vibrate (phones should be off during interviews)
- Watch alarm beeps
- Vehicle noises
- Animal sounds (birds, dogs, and so on)
- Jewelry rattling

If you're hearing something unpleasant while you're just sitting there conducting the interview, politely stop your subject (or just listen for a good break), then express your concerns to whoever's minding the audio.

Nine times out of ten, they'll catch it before you, but everyone spaces out once in a while and it's better safe than sorry.

Keeping Your Eyes Peeled

Just as there are plenty of audio issues that can ruin your interviews, there's also the chance that visual disturbances can screw up your material as well.[5]

Visual disturbances include, but are not limited to:

- Cast or crewmembers in shot
- Sudden shifts in lighting (with outdoor interviews, clouds can do odd things)
- Flies or bees in shot
- Weird items in interview area (camera batteries or tape left in view)
- Boom in shot
- Crazy flyaways in the subject's hair

"I once cut a show where the characters were so ill-spoken we had to cut together sentences as well as cut around some nose picking. Usually [bad interview] is just a result of dumb mistakes on the part of the interviewer. Frame your character correctly. Don't talk over a character. If it sounds okay once, get it again and better. Have your subject take off noisy jewelry. Ask all the questions on your list and at least three off the top of your head. It can mean the difference between a bite and a frankenbite."

—HEATHER J. MILLER, Co-Executive Producer, *Booze Traveler*

Keep 'em peeled out there, folks. While lots of interview is ultimately buried under picture, you should always help your crew get the best-looking/sounding material.

Sometimes, though, it's the cast members themselves that'll give you fits.

The Reluctant Subject

Despite the fact that folks sign on to appear in reality shows every day, you'll often find your subjects to be frightened, overly analytical about how they'll come off on camera, or completely teed off about how the experience isn't living up to their expectations. After all, they thought cameras would just be following them around and here's this production crew telling them where to be and what to do ten, twelve, sixteen hours a day for

---

5 Again, while your Camera Operator should be paying attention, sometimes you'll be the one who catches the goof.

weeks and months. At some point, some castmates just check out . . . and it's up to you and your field team to reel them back in and get the goods.

No matter what your characters' hang-ups, you're in trouble if you or your Field Producers can't come back with solid interview content. Here are a few tips and tricks to put cast members at ease . . . or at least get your content out of them.

Stammerers/Ramblers

Unsettled subjects often have a tendency to stammer or ramble. No matter how much you try to soothe them, they just can't seem to give you a clear or concise response.

The often well-meaning stammerers usually only trip over their words because they're in a hurry to respond to your questions. It's just a simple matter of their mouths getting ahead of their minds.

I've found that most stammerers can be cured by using what I call a "five count." Just explain to your subject that you'd like to be sure that your voices don't overlap on tape, and that they should mentally count to five before answering. Removing the pressure to respond immediately often does the trick.

Ramblers are a different breed. These folks couldn't deliver a complete, well-thought-out statement in an envelope. Their sentences run together, new thoughts are introduced in the middle of other thoughts, and it's virtually impossible to imagine their unfocused content ever making it to air.

Ramblers can be tamed by breaking your questions down. Instead of asking them to "tell us what happened when you got to the party," break it down into smaller bits like:

- "So, what were you thinking when you walked up to the door?"
- "What did Sara say to you when you went in?"
- "How did you react to Sara when she asked you that?"

Remember . . . it will all come together in post, so it doesn't matter if you get short answers. It's easier to put several thoughts together than it is to pull coherent content out of a rambling response.

The Victim / Self-Producer

Here's a real toughie. The Victim feels that he or she is being made to look bad based on their perception that the rest of the cast is turning against them. As a result, every interview encounter with them will register as another opportunity for you to embarrass or humiliate them.

Sample complaints from The Victim:

- "You guys are going to cut this up to make me look however you want, so I'm just not going to say anything."
- "You've been trying to make me look bad since day one."
- "I hate this place. I just want to go home."

The reason I also refer to Victims as "Self-Producers" is because, as you've read above, they'll frequently refuse to answer things or give you statements as written because they're sure it's just you looking for more ammo to blow holes in their personality on the show. They think that by managing everything they say in interview or do on screen that somehow they'll be able to control the end product.

Victims and Self-Producers are tough to work with, but setting aside some extra time in the interview to let them say anything they want to share outside of what you're asking them for can be helpful. It's not always a total write-off either — you often get great material out of letting them vent.

Attention, Blabbermouths!

A final consideration to remember in interview is to not leak information among the talent that other cast members have shared with you. If cast member X finds out from someone in-scene that cast member Y is talking about her behind her back, that's great TV. If she finds out from you during an interview, she's just had a realization off-camera — and you, my friend, will have a huge hole in your story.

Some Thoughts on Scenework

Whether you're safely ensconced in an un-air-conditioned garage somewhere in Encino in the middle of August watching house reality action go down or on location in Ohio taking notes on your cast lovebirds' romantic rowboat getaway at a mosquito-infested lake,[6] you're probably wondering why you're there instead of just watching whatever tape comes back at a later date. Well, here's why: Reality isn't just about rolling tape and waiting for happy accidents . . . sometimes you have to prod story along.

Stir It Up: Bringing Your Cast Back to Life

Just like in real life, there are moments of awkwardness or boredom during production in which cast members clam up and just stop talking to one another, and it's tough to squeeze story out of source material like a character reading a book on the couch while another one eats a hamburger across the room.

It's those duller moments that should prompt you to brainstorm with your Field Producers and figure out new ways to get your cast members talking, sparking conversations and debates that will further your story.

Take the cast members I just mentioned . . . the ones who are in the same room reading a book and eating a hamburger. Your Field Producer could be sent in to quietly suggest to one of the pair that they bring up the subject of last night's party, where one of the cast members fell in the pool during a fight with another cast member. Now you've gone from wasting tape waiting for action to happen to jump-starting genuine character interaction. Sure, the subject won't have come up organically, but you'll never know it in the final product. Once your fresh topic is off the blocks, your characters are suddenly talking again, and who knows what the new conversation may open up?

Feeding topics of conversation to your cast members during stagnant moments is just one way to liven things up without materially changing the agenda of the day's outline. Here are a few more:

- Suggest that a cast member privately reach out to another cast member who's withdrawing from interaction with the group.
- Ask some members of the cast to discuss (among themselves) who they feel is in the lead, getting the most attention, creating the most problems for the rest of the group, or who they're worried about losing to the next elimination.

---

6 I'm not overselling you on the glamour here, am I?

- If there's a good hour or two until the next planned activity in the outline, suggest a simple group activity that will put a sizable percentage of cast members in an immediate area and force interaction. Maybe an impromptu game of poker or a short soak in the hot tub will loosen their tongues.[7]

Take care, however, to not overwork your cast to the point where they start to resent being asked to instigate or participate in these little side moments.

Set Etiquette

While the world of reality production is often faster and looser than that of traditional scripted comedies and dramas, there are certain professional expectations during the production phase that are too important to be overlooked in this chapter.

Don't Feed the Animals:
The Talent Is Not Your Friend

You heard me.

The cast is not your friend. You are not their friend. You should try your best to get along with them on the rare occasions that you interact (during interviews, in odd situations where you're traveling together, and so on), but don't get chummy.

Why?

Once you lose your status as a disinterested observer in reality, the work suffers. Trust me. If your on-camera talent is making nonstop asides to the camera crew he's been playing cards with the night before[8] in the middle of a scene where he should be paying attention to a cast member, you'll either have to scrap the scenes or pray for a miracle in the edit bays.

Another rookie mistake is taking pictures with your cast members and posting them to your social networking site accounts. Remember way back when I told you how seriously reality producers, networks, and production companies take the illusion of reality? How do you think they'll react to seeing you and their talent doing shots together at a pub after a

---

7 If you can't get cast members to converse in a hot tub, hang up your reality hat.

8 True story.

"I was surprised by how unsleazy the producers were. These men and woman (yes, there was only one), and the entire crew, became my fast friends. I knew our friendship was fleeting (surely it wouldn't last beyond the few days we had together), but during our time waiting around for the lighting to be just right, or for someone to finish scouting a location ("Hurry up and wait," they would say), we had a lot of time to get to know one another. I buddied up to the Producers, some of the crew, and even my driver, a young college graduate who was my age. Once when we were driving, she referred to me as 'the talent.' 'Who?' I asked, thinking there might be a celebrity guest I didn't know about. 'That's you,' she said, 'you're the talent.'"[1]

—ANNA KLASSEN, Reality TV Participant and Entertainment Editor at www.Bustle.com

1 "I Was On Reality TV: Behind the Scenes Secrets of Faking Real Life," Anna Klassen, www.Bustle.com, 2/18/14.

day of shooting? You can, no kidding, be fired for this kind of behavior. I've seen the memos.

While we're on the subject of posting to social networking sites, it's even a bad idea for talent to have your email or social networking account info. Let's suppose that, months down the line, the show is on air and talent doesn't like what they see. They'll almost surely drop you an email or send you a private message asking you about what's coming up for them on the show, how they'll be portrayed later in the season, why you made certain choices with their content, or other questions along those lines. If you respond, you're likely in violation of your non-disclosure agreement, and discussing show content that hasn't aired yet with anyone, including cast, is a huge no-no. Giving a cast member written documentation about how you composed their scenework is about as wise as pouring gas on a fire. Last but not least, why lose valuable time and sleep over someone else's neuroses about how they're being portrayed on television, even if your characterization is spot-on?

In summation, getting chummy is a bad idea, though I certainly recommend making sure your talent feels that they're being handled with TLC, so that they don't go home regretting the decision to take on a reality show. Be kind, and learn the delicate balance between getting good content and being a good host to your TV "guests."

Trouble in Paradise:
What to Do When the Shoot Goes South

Few cast members truly realize what they've signed on for until things are underway for a few days. Most don't understand why the environments are so strictly controlled or why they're being directed to do or say specific things, and once the interaction with other cast members starts to get real, they may feel helpless and out of control as their expectations give way to the realities of participating in a reality program.

There's a tremendous amount of diplomacy and handholding to be done with reality cast members, and sometimes it falls on you to handle it. Remember, a cast member who feels manipulated and abused will create serious problems down the line and likely poison the attitudes of the whole group if left unchecked.

A Story Producer I know had the misfortune of sharing transportation a few times with a competitor on a reality series who was obsessed with pumping Producers and crew for information on her standing within the competition. No amount of encouragement, support, or information was enough for her, and when she was ultimately eliminated from the show, she was bitter and inconsolable, claiming that she felt "set up" because she couldn't get straight answers out of anyone during her experience.

I said this earlier, but it bears repeating: *Cast members are not your friends*, even though you should take measures to ensure that they're comfortable. I suggest you try to avoid dealing with them directly as much as possible and leave that to the Field Producers and faces they're familiar with. But when you can't avoid interaction (as with the instance in which that Story Producer had to share transportation), here are some things to remember:

- Never tell a cast member what will or won't be used on the show. If you're in the field, post may be making the call or the network may ask for the content you've told them wouldn't be used.[9]
- Never divulge to a cast member any information they haven't already learned on-set. And remember, talking to a cast member is like talking into a tape recorder that could be played back to anyone at any time.

---

9   Check with an EP if a cast member makes a special request, like removing a hurtful or legally questionable statement made by accident.

- Never tell a cast member how you think they're coming across on-camera in an effort to assuage them.
- Never tell an outright lie to a cast member to calm them. It's like setting a time bomb that'll eventually go off and obliterate any semblance of trust between them and the production.
- So with all those "nevers" laid down, what *can* you say?
- It's okay to tell them that your job prohibits you from having discussions with them about production . . . in fact, it's advisable.
- It's okay to tell a cast member that you empathize with their concerns, and that your focus is on telling a good story, not intentionally humiliating anyone.
- It's okay (and probably best) to deflect questions and major concerns to more senior Producers, Co-EPs, or EPs on set.

A Final Word on Production: Safety

Remember that the safety of your cast and crew takes precedence over getting story. If you overhear threats of bodily harm, cast revenge plots with a strong element of physical danger, or anything along those lines, report them to your superiors immediately.

If you think they won't take such threats seriously, guess again. During the taping of a major reality program some number of years ago, a cast member pressed a knife against a female castmate's throat, asking if it would "be okay if I killed you." The offending cast member was immediately ejected from the program. Reality gets enough bad press and criticism as it is for its dark side, and production companies aren't cruising for lawsuits.

While not all of them do, most production companies take the high road from the very beginning, subjecting potential participants to extensive psychiatric and character evaluations prior to adding them to the cast. I can speak firsthand to this as I was phoned as a reference for a friend who was to appear on a popular reality series just a few years ago. In the call, which lasted the better part of an hour, I was asked questions about my friend's typical alcohol consumption, propensity toward violence when provoked, and a host of other probing questions. It was really quite remarkable to experience just how thorough their process was.

In addition to psychological and character evaluations, hopefuls are also often given complete physical exams to ensure that they're up to the stress of appearing in reality programs with any sort of endurance considerations.

But enough about the cast. Let's talk about you and your health and safety.

You're on the same set in a complete run-and-gun environment for weeks at a time . . . and in your case, it's up to you alone to ensure that you're up to the challenge.

It's easy to forget the basics of keeping yourself physically and mentally well during production. Long days may mean lack of sleep, and you can't rely on production craft services to provide the most nutritious snacks or meal selections. After a few weeks of subsisting on nachos, chocolate candies, and soda, you're lucky to have any wits about you at all to handle story, so pack healthy, portable snacks at home and bring them to set if at all possible. Sleep as much as you can in the off-hours, and (if you can swing it) get a walk, a run, or a trip to the gym in every day to keep your energy up and provide the personal, reflective, regenerative downtime you need.

If you are being placed in a situation where you perceive you are at risk,[10] it's okay to say no to the production or ask if there's another member of the story team who doesn't feel as threatened or endangered by a situation. If the circumstances that may arise were not discussed at the time you were hired, you have every right to say no to risky activity. Above all, if you're asked to participate in illegal activity, you're well within your rights to refuse or walk away.

Remember: *No television show is worth your life, your health, your sanity, your freedom, or your safety.*

---

10 Accompanying cast members while zip-lining, whitewater rafting, rock climbing, or anything else that scares the pants off of you, for example.

Chapter Five Exercises

HOT SHEETS

Pick an exciting, action-packed day you and some friends have spent together in recent memory. Write up the action as a hot sheet, conveying the day's activities to someone who might need to know what happened that day in order to edit it. Use the good hot sheet example in this chapter as a guide. Remember, don't oversell the action!

INTERVIEW EXERCISE

Choose a friend or study partner and write a ten-question interview for them based on your knowledge of their lives. Make some of the questions mildly intrusive, on subjects they might not be prepared to discuss.

Now, interview your study partner. Can you put them at ease enough to get honest responses to the more intrusive questions?

Also, does your partner fall into any of the categories listed earlier in this chapter like the stammerer/rambler or self-producer? Did any of the techniques for handling them work, or did you find another approach that yielded the desired result?

SOCIAL MEDIA CHECK

Pick a handful of producers found in the credits of your favorite show and check out their Facebook pages. Do they even have one? Are the pages private? Are there many images of them with talent? Is there any content that you, as a network exec or employer, would find objectionable as far as references to the shows they work on?

Postproduction

"Having worked shows from preproduction through to the end, I personally prefer coming on as a post producer. I am a storyteller and my joy comes from taking a lump of raw footage and turning it into something people will want to watch."

—HEATHER J. MILLER, Co-Executive Producer, *Booze Traveler*

However you made it here, congratulations. It's either the first step of the last part of your journey or your first contact with material you'll be sweating over and swearing at for the next few weeks or months. If this stage is your first contact with the project, you'll likely be clenching your fists and stewing over one or more of these old welcome-to-post goof-up chestnuts:

"How could they not have covered that?"
"Was the sound guy asleep?"
"Who wrote these hot sheets?"

Before you fly completely off the handle, remember — hindsight is 20/20, and things get missed in the field no matter how good you or your team are. You can't fix *everything* in post, but your job now is to tell the best possible story with the content you've been given and under the conditions you've been asked to work.

Rethink Your Outline

Remember the episode outlines you (or your Producers / Field Producers) cooked up in preproduction? I'll wager a hearty handshake that half of that grand design went out the window in the field once story began to unfold. There's no way to completely predict the new story opportunities that will come up once the cameras start rolling or which planned events will fall flat, so it should come as no surprise that I suggest you use the first few days of post as a time for reevaluation.

The Big Picture

If you're working on a show whose main stories span a season rather than just separate individual episodes that are all self-contained, get the full run mapped out as far ahead as you can before you dive into the first episode. You're less likely to work yourself into a corner that way, and I've watched many an otherwise talented and efficient Story Producer chase rabbits down the wrong holes for weeks at a time by skipping this step. A day or two of sweating over the full season can save you a mess of trouble.

Remember back in preproduction when we had two of our surf show characters set themselves up as the nice guy and the villain? Now it's time to make sure that their journeys make sense.

First, consider each character's arc from the point we met them to the moment we left. Penny, our snobby surfboarding heiress, developed an unlikely friendship with a handsome surf bum (the very embodiment of what she had always hated about public beaches), learning some things about herself in the process and becoming someone we could actually root for. Frank, that character who came on the show to inspire others facing adversity after his post-accident return to surfing, rode his great attitude all the way to the semifinals, serving as a source of strength to everyone involved. That handsome surf bum that Penny fell for gave away one of his own boards to keep another player in the game, one who ultimately threw a surf-off in order to repay him the favor.

With any luck, you'll find after some analysis that you have a pretty jam-packed season of setups and payoffs, setups and payoffs. Sometimes, they're obvious, sometimes they may seem like you're stretching a wad of chewing gum to the moon, but look back and really map them out. No participant in a reality program is without a journey, even if that journey lands them right smack in the miserable place they started. Winning is a journey, just as trying and failing is . . . but how did your characters change and what did they learn?

Once you've beat out as many of these setups, payoffs, and character milestones as you can on index cards, arrange them to form the key moments within each episode of the season. It's that skeleton on which you can hang the meat of your show, episode by episode, avoiding the deadly trap of overloading early episodes with big action and not leaving anything dynamic for mid- to late-season episodes.

Keep It Meaningful, Keep It Moving

Now comes the tough part — fleshing out the episodes with scenes that embellish that basic structure you've created. Don't be afraid to go out of sequence in your timeline. If there's a great scene in which Frank and Penny argue over an omelet, it may not seem like much in its rough form. But insert it just before they have a major blowup on the beach and suddenly the omelet scene foreshadows the bigger event later. Throw in a bit of that evergreen interview content where other participants comment on Frank and Penny's growing resentment of each other, and the second scene of the beach becomes more powerful because it's contextualized.

It's important to understand that any content without purpose is nothing more than visual noise and can really slow down the sense that your story is chugging along. Every scene in your program should propel the story forward in a compact and effective way. Momentum matters!

The Return of the Forecast Bite

Earlier, I wrote about the importance of the forecast bite. As the show fills out and you start to see where you can put in your act breaks, these are the statements that will help you support dynamic ends to your acts, hooking viewers to come back for more. As innocuous as Frank and Penny's omelet scene at the end of an act may seem, underscoring it with a character stating "I'm pretty sure Frank and Penny both secretly want to drown each other" punctuated by a loud "I hate you" in-scene as Penny storms off at the end of an act is an explosion of action that will hook your audience into wanting to stick around.

So the Season's Mapped Out, Now What?

So you've translated the whole mess into a beautiful stack of outlines. Now what?

Your Supervising Producer, Executive Producer, and even the network folks may be the kind who would rather wait for a rough cut (the first pass at editing that takes you and your Editor a couple of weeks to bang out) to start offering notes and asking why the story they're watching in the edit bay doesn't match the one they thought they'd be seeing.

That's why it's critical, especially under reality's usual time constraints, to pass along those outlines you've just created as soon as they're ready.

My revised outlines are usually formatted like the following example. The parenthetical "A" and "B" markings here indicate content relating to my "A" story (the main story) and "B" story (a second supporting story), a practice I've adopted to ensure at a glance that my bases are covered. Sometimes, I'll go so far as to add a "C" story if there are only a few beats to something funny or interesting.

TIP Create a new outline and submit it to your superiors even if you're not asked for one. This extra step, though most Supervising Producers don't request it, can save you days of re-editing and trying to explain why things didn't happen or why they were poorly executed.

"BEACHES" EPISODE 101

A story: start of competition, rivalries established
B story: Jill and Dana leave for different reasons

ACT ONE

1. Surfers Meet, Get Room Assignments (A)
2. First Surf Flagler Beach (A)
3. The Surf Safety Test (A)
4. Surfers Guess Their Closest Competition Is (A)
5. Frank Teaches a Traditional Dance, Befriends Jill (B)
6. Jill Tells Mary Her "Big Secret" (B)
7. Frank and Penny Midnight Omelet Argument, Sets Up Frank Versus Penny (A)

ACT TWO

1. Balance Challenge (A/B)
2. Girls Reassess Their Competition with Host (A)
3. Host Tells the Girls to Get Ready to Surf (A)
4. Jill Is Leaving (A/B)
5. The Contest (A/B)
6. Dana Wants to Leave (B)
7. The Big Powwow (B/A)

ACT THREE

1. Penny Rips on Dana in Front of the Other Girls (B)
2. Host Announces That Jill and Dana Are Leaving Now (A/B)
3. Jill and Dana Leave (B)
4. Penny Gloats Over Dana's Departure, Frank Vows to Defeat Penny (B/A)

As with all television, the "A" story is the main thrust of the episode, and the "B" or "C" stories are important to either maintain a storyline that's taken a backseat for an episode or two or to just plain give us a break from the "A" story once in a while. "B" stories are also where I usually like to hide my humor in otherwise tense or dramatic programs or, conversely, hide my serious or touching content in an otherwise comedic program.

Pay attention to the length of each act (usually four minutes at the low end to fourteen minutes at the longest, dictated by the network but with a little wiggle room in most cases) and consider both how much information you're getting across and how easy the story is to follow. Your audience will have to contend with everything from the kids crying in the next room to noisy commercial breaks.

As someone who loves story and hates repetition, that last bit of advice broke my heart when I started in reality TV. It's true, though. If a viewer can't walk away to check on the soup pot in the kitchen and come back to the show fully understanding what's happening even after they've missed a minute or two, you've failed.

Identify your strongest story each episode, augment it with strongly delineated B and C storylines, and you should be okay.

A Word on Stakes

As you compose your show, whether on paper or with an editing system, be mindful of the stakes in each scene. A bunch of talking heads are meaningless if they're not advancing the story. Every cast member wants or needs something, and every scene should drive the story forward by hitting home what's at risk for each person.

Stakes don't always shout themselves out. Sometimes they whisper. Some examples of stakes that shout:

- A cast member must complete a challenge in order to achieve immunity.
- A group prepares to vote on who should stay or go in a competition.
- A player must excel in order to defeat teammates who have aligned against her.

In all of these examples, it's pretty easy to see what the consequences will be for anyone who fails to succeed. But what about less obvious stakes? The ones that whisper?

Here are a few of that variety:

- A cast member struggles to overcome self-doubt and generate some self-esteem.
- A character risks embarrassment by agreeing to attempt something awkward.
- A character must decide whether telling the truth is worth losing an ally.

None of the above "whispered" stakes have game-ending consequences. Well, at least not immediate ones. But they keep viewers engaged just as the more obvious examples do.

If your source material is looking a little weak, there are a few tricks in your magic story bag that can be called upon. Here are a few devices that sometimes work, though I'm not advocating that you use them indiscriminately:[1]

The Ticking Clock

Oh, no! This couple only has three days to finish renovating their entire house in order to have it ready for a Realtor to show!

Really? Would you ever put yourself under that kind of ludicrous stress, scheduling an open house three days after you decide to completely gut your house? More likely than not, this is a fabrication created by the show's Producers and story team to add urgency to otherwise mundane things like completing a checklist of the "repaint / refinish / hang drapes" variety.

Other more subtle examples might include getting a pickup interview with a cast member to grab a few fabricated lines like: "I really wanted to finish this before Ted got home," or "If I don't get this place cleaned up in a hurry, Sheila's gonna kill me."

Inserting a ticking clock into a show is dangerous business, as they're one of the most easily identifiable cheats around.

---

1 Applied carelessly, these can cost you the trust of your audience.

The Big Deal Out of Nothing

Let's say we're doing a fitness show about a bunch of people who have to complete physical challenges to win points, and the current challenge is running up and down a massive flight of stairs in a building.

The cast member who's currently leading the pack on the show accidentally sprains his ankle, effectively eliminating himself from the event, even though he's in no danger of leaving the show. On set, he's taken off to one side to be examined by an emergency medical technician (most physical challenge shows have an EMT on set). He then ices down his ankle while the rest of the team completes the task.

Disappointing, sure. But get creative with your interview bites with other cast members afterward, show him with the EMT, throw in a shot of an ambulance, and suddenly you've got people worrying what went wrong and whether or not he'll have to leave the show as a result of his unspecified injury.

Sure, you can't sustain the illusion for long (you'll have to reveal the "just a sprained ankle" sooner than later to avoid ticking your audience off), but this kind of manufactured suspense makes for one heck of an act break.

The Repurposed Scene

Here's a tricky one in which you'll need to take an entire scene and create a false subtext. Let's say you have a scene that looks like this, transcribed in two-column AV format for illustration:

VIDEO	AUDIO
1003A04 14:00:10 Jill enters the club. She finds Katherine at a table and sits down.	1003A04 14:00:10 Jill: "Hi, Katherine. Thanks for meeting me."
1003A04 14:00:25 Katherine and Jill eye each other for a moment.	1003A04 14:00:25 Katherine: "So, who do you think we should ask to go to the big charity event? Jill: "I have a few ideas."
1003A04 14:02:05 Jill and Katherine talk.	1003A04 14:02:05 Katherine: "How about Joan?" Jill: "Sure, fine by me."
1003A04 14:10:08 Katherine excuses herself.	1003A04 14:10:08 Katherine: "So I'll call Joan and let her know she's invited."

Pretty innocuous content. But let's see what happens to it when you add some more biting interview content left over from a confrontation Katherine and Jill had about Katherine leaving her toothbrush and toothpaste out a week prior.

VIDEO	AUDIO
1003A04 14:00:10 Jill enters the club. She finds Katherine at a table and sits down.	1003A04 14:00:10 Jill: "Hi, Katherine. Thanks for meeting me."
0928C04 16:09:19 Interview content: Jill	0928C04 16:09:19 JILL: THE THING ABOUT KATHERINE IS THAT SHE'S OBLIVIOUS TO THE FACT THAT SHE JUST MAKES PEOPLE CRAZY.
1003A04 14:00:25 Katherine and Jill eye each other for a moment.	1003A04 14:00:25 Katherine: "So, who do you think we should ask to go to the big charity event? Jill: "I have a few ideas."
0928C09 21:15:13 Interview content: Katherine	0928C09 21:15:13 KATHERINE: JILL ALWAYS WANTS THINGS DONE HER WAY. WHICH IS WHY I'M OFFICIALLY MAKING IT MY GOAL TO GET HER THROWN OFF THE SHOW. NOT THAT I'M GOING TO TELL HER THAT.
1003A04 14:02:05 Jill and Katherine talk.	1003A04 14:02:05 Katherine: "How about Joan?" Jill: "Sure, fine by me."
0928C04 16:11:10 Interview content: Jill	0928C04 16:11:10 JILL: YECCH.
1003A04 14:10:08 Katherine excuses herself.	1003A04 14:10:08 Katherine: "So I'll call Joan and let her know she's invited."

What you've just done is taken an innocuous bit of spare content, added leftover bites from an incident about a messy bathroom, and created a cut-from-whole-cloth scene about how these two women, beneath their cheery facades, can't stand each other.

Like I said . . . I don't advocate this kind of heavy-handed stuff, but if it passes your ethical gut check, it'll give your sense of drama a shot in the arm. My own rule of thumb is that as long as no one is doing something out of character or saying something that's not in keeping with their usual take on things, it's worth considering.

Composing a Stringout

A "stringout" is a loose visual assembly of scenework, dialogue, and sometimes B-roll that is used by Editors as the loose foundation for their work. These can be created in two different ways — by creating a written edit called a "paper cut" that Assistant Editors can assemble into a stringout for the Editor, or by bypassing the Assistant Editors and assembling it yourself using an editing system.

Option One: The Paper Cut

While most companies have made the change to providing you, the Story Producer, with Final Cut Pro or Avid systems to string out material before turning it over to your Editor, a few holdouts still require Story Producers to execute "paper cuts," script-like edits that are passed along to an Assistant Editor to assemble.

You may be asked to format these differently from job to job, but here's a fragment of how I usually write mine in the good old two-column AV format you saw earlier, complete with narrative voice over (or V.O.) in caps:[2]

---

2 See Appendix B for tips on writing great V.O. and host copy.

ACT ONE

VIDEO	AUDIO
103010A03 11:10:30 – 11:10:40 Fred herds the gang into the minivan.	VO: TODAY'S TRIP TO THE HOLLY-WOOD WALK OF FAME MIGHT JUST BE THE LAST STRAW FOR FRED.
103010A03 11:25:30 – 11:25:40 The group van cruises out of the driveway.	103010B01 10:15:05 Fred OTF: *"Today we're all going to the Hollywood Walk of Fame for a challenge."*
>>>>>>>>>>>>>>>>>>>>>>	103010A03 11:38:10 – 11:39:38 Fred tells Ricky that he hates being out in public, because he hates talking to fans.
103010A03 11:41:02 – 11:41:07 Ricky rolls his eyes at Fred.	103010B05 12:15:09 Ricky OTF: "I've never known anybody so self-centered. // ~~Fred is just . . . . I don't know.~~ // Fred's always dissing our fans, and who are we without our fans?"

You'll notice a few things about this entry.

Each clip begins with the source tape number (like 103010A03, which would indicate October 30, 2010), the camera (Camera A), that camera's tape number (03, the third tape for that camera that day), and is followed by time code (11:25:30 in the morning). This is what your Assistant Editor is primarily concerned with when assembling the stringout.

If there's one thing an Editor hates, it's receiving a stringout for an eight- or ten-minute act that's thirty or forty minutes long. With the two-column paper cut, it's easy to guesstimate the length of your stringouts to within a minute or two.

I don't usually include end times on interview or OTF content entries (as in, "12:15:09 – 12:15:20") because when you've got a literal transcription of something stated, it will be pretty obvious to the Assistant Editor when it ends, which is not the case with in-scene action. I might include an "out time" on interview/OTF content if the person made a weird or interesting expression at the end of their statement that I'd like to see make the cut, but otherwise, just an "in time" will do.

Check out the bit of OTF dialogue from Ricky in the last frame of the sample. If you have a single sentence or two of interview/OTF that you'd like to see omitted in the final stringout, just set it apart with forward slashes and strike through it. It's much less stressful for you and your Assistant Editor to strike through content than dice it into multiple single entries. In other words, there's no reason to go this crazy:

VIDEO	AUDIO
103002A03 11:41:02 – 11:41:07 Ricky rolls his eyes at Fred.	103002B05 12:15:09 Ricky OTF: "I've never known anybody so self-centered."
103002A03 >>>>>>>>>>>>>>>>>>>>>	103002B05 12:15:17 Ricky OTF: "Fred's always dissing our fans, and who are we without our fans?"

It's only a couple of seconds . . . don't go nuts!

If you're using the mostly outdated paper cut technique as part of your workflow, be sure to provide a copy of the document to your Editor even though he or she will be working primarily from a stringout. It's useful to your Editor if your intentions are ever in question or if your stringouts aren't executed exactly as you'd asked of your Assistant Editor, which can happen.

Now about that voiceover content in paper edits: Keep it simple. Too floral, too clever, too precious in the beginning? Don't make the mistake of thinking that your voiceover copy is there to shout through the reality clutter to tell the world you're a literate writer, even if the mouthfuls of alliterative and cutesy turns of phrase kill the person who eventually has to read them. Remember, too, that V.O. should be used for setting things up, filling in blanks, or guiding your viewers to react as you desire . . . not to merely reiterate what you're already seeing on screen.

> "A lot of story folk come from writing backgrounds, and many of them are quite literary. They often write too flowery or have too many SAT words that will never survive the notes process. You wrote one of the best pieces of V.O. I have heard: 'While Wayne's team is coming together, Gerald's is falling apart.' It's simple, accessible, and easy to understand. But it's also observant, and a bit profound."
>
> — **ERIC ANDERSON**, Editor

Option Two: The Avid / Final Cut Pro Stringout

Every single show I've worked on in the past five years now provides its story team with workstations on which to compose first-pass stringouts of story material. The last show I didn't have my own workstation on was in 2013, while overseeing a group of Story Producers who all had their own workstations.

Yes, the game has changed for good in reality television. Where story skills were once enough for Story Producers, the tools and workflow have changed to a point where if you are not fluent in Final Cut Pro or Avid, your opportunities are seriously diminished.

Caps for emphasis, dear reader: YOU ARE GOING TO HAVE TO LEARN TO EDIT.

If you don't have any film school friends who can teach you the basics, many community colleges and universities offer basic editing courses at nominal fees.

The chief benefits of creating your own stringouts in Avid or Final Cut Pro are:

- You can work at an accelerated pace and to see how your story is (or isn't) coming together in a way that you can't with old-school paper cuts.
- If your source materials are grouped (meaning all available camera angles are available to view in a split-screen grid), you'll save a lot of time knowing what will and won't work by seeing the complete picture.
- You can more clearly articulate how you'd like the final product to look.

Remember when executing your stringout that you are *not* the Editor. The stringout should not contain dissolves or complicated cuts. The stringout exists only to efficiently represent the mechanics of your story to the Editor, whose job is, in turn, to take your coarse assembly and turn it into a visually pleasing end result.

> "The story staff I enjoy working with is one that wants to work as a team — and by team, I mean not the 'Story Producer team' or the 'Editor team' but all of us as a team. Without that mentality in place, it becomes a battle of who thinks they know the show better."
>
> — **MARK CEGIELSKI**, Editor

Now what about the V.O. content you'd have normally written into a paper cut? Or the interview content and pickup scenes that you have asked for but not yet received from the field?[3] Well, you've got a couple of choices. You can use the editing system's title tool to create "cards" that you can drop into the spots where the anticipated content should go, or simply use locators or note features (unique to each editing system) to indicate materials expected for later.

As for host voice over, typically recorded late in the process, provide your Editor with a hard copy of that missing material that they can "temp

---

3 Yes, it happens. With the compressed schedules nowadays, you can be in post while the field is still shooting.

in" using the microphone typically found in reality edit bays.[4] Composing the printed list saves your Editor the trouble of scrolling through your stringout to find material one chunk at a time, and will give you a base for the V.O. script you'll have to pass on to your host talent to read later.

In addition to my stringouts, I often create what I call "junk bins" in my Avid projects. In these bins, I save extraneous scenework and moments that I find interesting but not necessarily in service of the story I've chosen to tell.

Why save them? Because being able to show your Supervising Producer or Editor why something doesn't work is easier than having to go back and waste time constructing a flawed scene just to prove it doesn't work. Also, having an extra scene at your fingertips can save you and your Editor from a last-minute scramble for material if your show comes up a few minutes short.

Here's another good reason to maintain your junk bins: Often, you'll be asked (with very little notice) to provide "bonus" scenes or other content that can be used to promote your show online. Also, some programs may require additional superfluous scenes called "snap-ins," so named for the way they are inserted into the program in order to elongate episodes for broadcast outside the US where there's less advertising time in each broadcast hour.

If you've got plenty of extra material in your junk bins, you'll always be ahead of the game.

A Word on Act Breaks

An "act break" is the moment between acts in which, most often, your show will be going to a commercial. It's crucial to remember that during those breaks, your viewers will often be surfing other channels.[5] You absolutely must end each act with some sort of dramatic, unresolved bit of business to draw them back.

One neat trick that keeps viewers engaged is breaking a scene at a critical moment and then returning to the same scene following the act break. Let's say Act Two of your show ends with a huge fight. Rather than

---

4 Temporary audio helps you to better guess program length and brings the show to life in early screenings with your coworkers and superiors in a way that cards can't.

5 Even in this age of DVR, when viewers often record their shows and speed through the commercials on playback, commercial breaks still trigger the question "Do I want to keep watching this?"

> "The most difficult story people that I come across are essentially either too lazy, or at the other end of the spectrum, too motivated. The former tend to just find a shot that's good enough. They try to sell you on using the first thing they come across that will kind of work. Their mantra is 'good enough, let's move on and get this thing done.' The overly motivated types are usually careerists who don't want to be on the story rung of the career ladder anymore. They are going to ride their Editors like rented mules to deliver them to a producing job. I have to say that for the most part, I have been fortunate to get good people most of the time . . . the ones who collaborate and keep it light and funny, giving you space to be creative and helping when it's needed."
>
> **— ERIC ANDERSON**, Editor

resolve the fight, then see the fallout, then cut to commercial with nothing to entice your audience to return, look for the most dramatic moment to halt the action mid-scene, creating a solid "out."

For example: Character "Bill" pulls a cake out of the refrigerator and declares in interview that he's going to teach character "Mike" a lesson. Boom. End Act Two right there. Act Three can then resume with a castmate's recap of what just happened followed by the completion of the action — smashing the cake into Mike's face to the screeching delight of the other castmates.

From there, you can then finish the scene and move on to the next.

Teases

Another device at your disposal for audience retention is the "tease." A tease is a short glimpse at a dramatic moment in the next act or, in the case of a "deep tease," a noisy or emotional major moment from even later in the episode.

Typically, I don't sweat teases until later in the rough cut process, as so much can change or be reordered between the time you execute your new outline, initial stringout, and the completion of the first "rough cut," the loose first pass you and your Editor will collaborate on.

The Rough Cut

So your paper script or stringout is complete . . . congratulations! Now, let's run it through the meat grinder we call the "rough cut."

Even since the first publication of this book in 2011, rough cuts have begun to look more and more like nearly finished episodes. Where they once were used as a thumbnail sketch of where story was headed, they're now almost as polished as a finished show.

As you settle in, be sure that you and your Supervising Producer and EPs are on the same page about what they are expecting to see. Does that outline I asked you to write for them — the one they didn't ask for — make sense to them? Then proceed.

With your paper cut and/or subsequent stringout ready, you may now commence with the sweet experience of being locked in a dark room with an Editor for weeks knocking out that rough cut . . . or so you'd think. Every Editor I've ever worked with would probably agree with the next bit of advice I'm about to give you: *Get things started, then get out.*

That's right, *get out.* Don't hover. The last thing an Editor needs is an edit bay buddy watching their every move. But before you close the door behind you, make sure you've reviewed materials with your Editor and communicated your basic expectations and the intent of each scene.

But how will you know what's going on if you're not there, staring down every keystroke, snip, and effect? What if the Editor doesn't follow your script to the last detail? What if they blow open your precious script or stringout and start adding or changing things? Well, all of that could happen, but there's at least a 50% chance that their creative input will improve on your work. Keep an eye on the schedule, drop in just a couple of times a day and ask what they might need, but stay out of their hair the

> "As we start going through the material, it would be best if, right away, before we even start looking — you tell us what you are looking for, what directives you have from the executives. We are here to help you, and we also want the best story possible and to make your life easier. Some Editors need more guidance than others. While viewing material, 'story' pops out for some Editors; others need to be told more specifically what to look for. Are you looking for relationship? Humor? Drama? Process? What are your goals and hopes with this material that we are about to look at? What have you been told by the Field Producers? Share your insights with us. This will help us give you what you want. It will also help us to cut faster and wade through what is probably hours and hours of footage. Gems can slip by if we don't know what they look like."
>
> — PAM MALOUF, Editor

"My friend James was in town and wanted to come and visit me at work. He was wide-eyed and impressed with the whole place and all the shows that get done there. He watched us work together for a while, and then when I went to lunch with him he asked who was in charge. I did not know what he meant. He asked our job titles. I said Lead Editor and Supervising Story Producer. He asked which one was higher than the other, because he saw you pull a couple shots for me, and then I cut something the way you wanted it. And then we kind of workshopped some V.O. together. He said he couldn't tell who was running the cut. I thought, hmm . . . that's probably a very good thing. I answered that I didn't know the answer to his question, and that it really didn't matter. What matters is how good the show comes out. I think that's an example of a stellar Story Producer / Editor work relationship, and a recipe for success."

— ERIC ANDERSON, Editor

first few days. Establish trust. Show them you're not a maniac about having your scripts followed to the letter.

Remember, your job is to create and distill story. The Editor's job is to refine that story into an engaging audiovisual end product. The working relationship and distribution of creative labor once your story hits the edit bay is up to the two of you to hammer out.

When your Editor's ready to show you something (which should be within the first few days), be as positive as you can. Worry about the big picture more than whether or not you like minor visual choices. Is your story intact? Did they improve on your work? Does the story feel like it's moving?

Remember that yours is a collaborative partnership. If something isn't working, don't attack your Editor in a "Hey, you're messing this up" tone. Ask them if something might work better if variables X or Y were to change or suggest that their ideas might not be in total sync with the style of the program. A little diplomacy goes a long way.

If they're dismissive or completely bullheaded about your input, though, take action sooner than later.

If the Editor has worked at the production company for a long period of time or has a history with the Supervising Producer, any of the Executive Producers, or (heaven forfend) the owners of the company, approach the Supervising Producer about how best to rectify the situation. Don't fly into their office yelping about how so-and-so won't work with you or do what you're asking them to do. Just ask (calmly) if they've worked with the Editor before and if they have any advice on how to handle them diplomatically. I once worked with an Editor who was prone to bouts of explosive frustration with our not-always-so-great source material, so once every four hours, I'd drop by and ask him if he wanted to walk to the corner store with me to get a diet soda or just to take a lap around the block. That was all it took to refocus and refresh him, and now he's one of the go-to guys I recommend almost every time I'm allowed to hire my own team.

Usually within two to four weeks (depending on your circumstances), you and your Editor will have a rough cut ready to screen internally to your Supervising Producer and/or Executive Producer. It should be just a few minutes longer than your show's target run time. My rule of thumb is nothing should screen at more than 10% over target . . . a rough cut for forty minutes of content, for me, should screen at no longer than forty-four minutes. Rough cuts that are too short will seem skimpy and beg the question, "Is that all we had?" Conversely, a rough cut that screens too long brings up questions about whether you and your Editor know how to tell your story efficiently.

It's important during the rough cut screening and notes process to avoid becoming irrationally defensive about your choices or selling your Editor down the river when one of their decisions raises an eyebrow. If something is missing from the rough cut, either because you opted not to use certain source material or because your Editor deleted it, be prepared to helpfully explain why it's been omitted. Sound confident, but don't be afraid to say "I'll review the material again" if something that didn't make the cut is asked for. It's not the Spanish Inquisition, it's just a screening — so stay calm.

Once you've got your internal notes on the rough cut, it's time to move on to the next step.

The Rough Cut Goes to Network: First Notes

After your internal screening for your immediate superiors, your rough cut will be ready to send to network. Brace yourself, as here come the network notes![6]

---

6 If you get to the end of this and decide you want to go deeper into how the notes process works, see my short e-book *And Another Thing* on Amazon.

You've probably heard or read a lot of funny stories about network notes. My all-time favorite is (and I'm only lightly paraphrasing it here): "Thank you for so thoroughly addressing our notes. Show is now boring for some reason. What can we do about this?"

It's easy to laugh or cry or get worked up over network notes, but remember — this is their first contact with your material and these are the folks footing the bill for your show and its promotion in hopes that it'll be engaging enough to attract advertisers, awards, and other returns on their costly investment. Of course they want to have some input on what will be going out on their network!

A good exec will likely pass back a lot of notes like these:

"Can we see/hear more of Alice in interview after the pool incident? Good content."

"Conflict seems weak. Would flashing back to Joe's past failures raise the stakes?"

"Act Three moves slowly. We could probably live without the scene in the kitchen."

What makes these notes easily addressable is the fact that every one maps out a solution the exec thinks will help the project along. There's careful consideration of the work going on here, and whether you agree or disagree with the notes, the unwritten subtext here is "do your best to achieve X, Y and Z and I'll probably approve the cut."

You and your Supervising Producer may wish to "push back" on a note or two that everyone feels strongly about, but as with all creative work, it helps to pick your battles rather than reject changes out of hand. You don't know what kind of odd pressures your network execs are up against or what motivates them to ask for certain changes, so it's best to cut them some slack and not simply regard them as the enemy, a reflexive state of mind that you'll need to learn to control if you plan to stick around in reality TV.

Now, just as there are talented, thoughtful, capable execs out there who can really help you out by seeing your work with fresh eyes, there are also a handful that should really get out of the business and consider managing a mop factory. They're the ones who either review shows in a hurry or pawn off the responsibility of giving notes to their assistants, in which case your fate now rests in the hands of a twenty-two-year-old with $400 shoes and an Ivy League degree in English who's biding their time until they can transform, butterfly-like, into an exec themselves.

Notes from these somnambulist execs or their assistants often read like this:

"This needs to be better."

"Act Two is boring."

"Have Hank *(insert impossible, unmotivated thing character did not do and that cannot be picked up)* somewhere near the end of Act Three."

Note the complete absence of any suggested course of action save for the third note, which fails to explain the motivation behind the weird addition even while knotting your eyebrows as to how you can make a specific thing happen long after your tape's been shot and the gang's gone home.

When execs hand you lemons, make lemonade. If there's absolutely no way to get around a clinker of a note, there are three remedies that (usually) work.

First, you and your superiors can push back on the note, respectfully disagreeing and supporting the decision with an easily absorbed explanation like "material does not exist" or "change is likely to undermine the punch of the payoff in Act Five." Language should not challenge the merit of the note, only why the change cannot (or should not) be made.

Second, you can address their notes to the letter and let the exec realize on their own that the suggestion doesn't work. I've never liked this approach, as it's passive-aggressive, a colossal waste of time, and there are no guarantees that the exec will actually realize that anything's been made worse as a result of their note. It's risky.

Third, you can come at it as I most often do: Make changes based on the "spirit" of the notes, which is my fancy way of saying that there's no way to address them except by sleight of hand. By that, I mean that you, your Editor, and your Supervising Producer can probably survive them by changing a few music cues, compressing an act to create enough room for a short scene you initially deleted (making the action more dense), or peppering in a few more reaction shots or side comments. Your annotated replies to these notes, which usually accompany your next output in written form, should look something like this:

For "This needs to be better," respond with "Act improved significantly by use of more upbeat music cues and minor revisions to scenework."

For "Act Two is boring," tell them you "Revised scenework to quicken pace."

For the impossible action request, try "Reviewed source material, but found no such action. However, added X and Y to draw more focus to Hank."

See that? You've materially changed the episode and supported your decisions by suggesting how this largely meaningless shuffling should be interpreted, which registers to the note giver as respecting/addressing their notes. Yes, with a bit of good luck, your less-experienced, less-articulate exec or their pet assistant will feel that they're being listened to and that'll be that.

Most often, networks ask for more than one review, so your new version will be output and sent back to them, where the refinement process continues (sometimes after multiple rough cut passes) with the "fine cut."[7]

The Fine Cut

Once the network has exhausted their agreed-upon number of rough cut passes, you and your Editor will attempt to address the notes you've been given while tightening the cut as closely as possible to the exact length at which it will air.

The fine cut will include final graphics and more closely approximate the product the viewer will see. Your Editor will be busy addressing music, graphics, and other non-story notes in addition to making the changes you provide, so as with all stages of post, don't micromanage them.

The Locked Cut

Once the network signs off on your edited-to-time final cut, it's time to lock the cut. You and you Editor may still need to tweak the show to *exact* time before passing the show off to the Online Editor, who will be responsible for color correcting the show, remixing the audio, and sweating the small stuff that makes your product airable.

Once that's completed, congratulations! Weeks or months of hard work later, you've finally finished an episode!

---

7 No guarantees. Some request multiple rough or fine cut passes.

A Special Word on Series and Season Premieres and Finales

One great truth about post: Series and season premieres will take longer to fine-tune 99% of the time than regular episodes, so be ready. Series and season premieres and finales often require a lot of additional fiddling to get just right, so you'll often be asked to take more passes at these internally before they go to network, and will probably receive heavier-than-usual notes once they do.

This is normal, as most execs seem to be laser-focused on great premieres and the first two episodes following every season, as that's when they are most concerned about viewer engagement. A so-so premiere that fails to hook an audience equals disaster for the series on the whole. No viewer is going to stick around until Episode Four to decide if they like something.

What should you pay the most attention to in a series or season premiere?

One of the most time-consuming and difficult parts of any series premiere is the introduction of cast. While we talked about this earlier when we went over how to conduct great profile interviews, the subject of establishing cast bears revisiting in post, as that's where your stories are boiled down.

We've got to meet everyone in the episode, and while it's important to get those personalities across, you can't do it at the expense of story, which also has to kick into gear pretty quickly.

In the first season of *Basketball Wives*,[8] for example, the show opens with a sensational "Tonight On"[9] to hook viewers. In just thirty seconds or so, it establishes that the show takes place in glamorous South Beach, Evelyn's still teary about her breakup, Gloria and Shaunie have unspoken tension because Gloria's sister was rumored to have slept with Shaunie's ex-husband, and Royce's outrageous dance moves at a party somewhere in the episode come as a shock to the others, establishing her as a wild card in the group.

---

8 *Basketball Wives* Episode 101, as of this edition's publication, can still be found online at VH1.com for review and analysis.

9 The short highlights reel that runs at the very top of an episode that shows what's on tonight's episode.

More than just teasing story, a Tonight On is a quick snapshot of cast dynamic that informs the background packages seen in the first act. It's your first opportunity to give viewers a taste of your cast, so make it count!

Let's continue with the *Basketball Wives* analysis, moving on into the first act just after the Tonight On and opening titles.

At the top of the first act, Shaunie O'Neal has arrived in Miami and calls to get some of the other wives together for dinner and drinks. This gets the entire cast together in the same room, providing a natural bed for the background packages even as the anticipation surrounding Gloria's arrival at the restaurant foreshadows what could be an uncomfortable interaction with Shaunie.

By the end of the first act, the entire core cast has been introduced in that restaurant scene, leaving only Jennifer's background package to run at the top of Act Two as drinks and dinner progress. Suzie is introduced in later acts, but as her function in the first episode is mostly supporting, she's not given an especially in-depth introduction.

If you can get your cast introduced and still end your first act on a real cliffhanger (in this case, what might happen when Shaunie and Gloria get together), those stakes alone should alleviate a lot of concern about the show's pacing, one of the most common notes you'll receive internally and from network.[10]

While we're on the subject of first episodes, especially important in a series premiere are the establishment of the "series thesis" and each cast member's "character thesis," which tell viewers what the heart of the show is and direct them to watch for further developments on specific fronts for each player, respectively.

Going back to *Basketball Wives*, Shaunie's first appearance (backed by a song whose lyrics include "I can make it on my own") covers the full cast: "It may seem like Basketball Wives have it all, but I know for a fact that the glamour, the glitz, the attention, it all comes with a price. Behind the bling, we deal with all types of craziness, from cheating, to groupies, to loneliness. Although our lives are crazy and all over the place, I think it's important that we stick together and make it through as a team." This is, essentially, the series thesis. Will these women be able to stick together and support each other through whatever may come?

---

10   Remember: Every act should end with a cliffhanger or anticipation of an upcoming action.

In *Basketball Wives*, the show established in the first acts that Jennifer is on the verge of divorce, Royce is worried about how she's perceived in the community (supported by interview content from Evelyn and Jennifer, who are suspicious of her despite Shaunie wanting to take her in), Shaunie finds Gloria a bit of a young know-it-all who thinks her marriage is perfect and doesn't know what she's in for, and so on. You know exactly what to watch for in the early episodes from these character theses, and the first episode pays off the thesis about Royce's supposed messiness/immaturity as Evelyn and Jennifer host an image intervention for her after her wild dance moves raise eyebrows at a poolside event.

Again, I mention this in the section on post, as you won't be shooting in the field with much thought about act breaks or structure beyond nailing groups of beats that will eventually become story. Dividing content to meet the act lengths dictated by network isn't anything to sweat in the field.[11]

A Special Word on Postproduction Etiquette

Have you ever heard the phrase "We'll fix it in post?" It's often heard on sets where traditionally scripted content is made, but it's also common in reality television. Sometimes, you're really being called upon to work a lot of magic in a very short period of time. With budgets and schedules often constricted in attempts to offset cost overruns in production, it's easy to feel pressure when the circumstances aren't ideal.

You may run into situations like these:

- The music library your show is assigned doesn't work well for the material.
- The field is not responding to pickup requests from post in a timely manner.
- Field notes are absent or several days delayed.
- Material to be edited is not being ingested into the system quickly enough to be reviewed by the post-based story team, or is not properly grouped, making it impossible for the story team to create stringouts to pass along to Editors.
- Editors are discarding stringouts and cutting material from scratch rather than working with the story team.

---

11 That being said, it never hurts to add the phrase "possible act out" in your field notes if something noteworthy and powerful happens.

There are a host of issues unique to post that can make it a stressful place to be. This is why it's important to remember, for the sanity and work relationship of the team, you'll need to keep it together and not fall into a routine of making complaints or becoming a downer. Raise issues, but only in order to call them to the attention of your immediate supervisor.

When calling an issue to the attention of your immediate supervisor, it's usually best to send them an email about it first, then use email to follow up on your understanding of the conversation as you implement whatever strategy is requested of you.

For example:

To: Fred.Example@productioncompanyexample.com
From: Hank.Whatshisname@productioncompanyexample.com
Subject: Music library

Fred,
I've been discussing the music library with the Editors, and we are in agreement that most of the tracks available to us are either too over-the-top comedic or over-the-top dramatic. Would it be possible for us to get some more general-use cues?
Thanks,
Hank

There's another reason to keep email records of your interactions with your superiors. On occasion, disputes may arise as to what had been discussed and shared, and it's helpful to be able to pull up those old emails to remind them of the direction you'd received or to defend yourself in the odd case where someone might claim you never informed them about an issue, putting responsibility for costly delays and errors on you.

While it's important to be a team player in every stage of the process, you've really got to keep it together in post. That said, you've also got to cover yourself by being as sure as possible that you and your superiors are on the same page. If you can pull that off, you should be able to turn out great show after great show with as little friction as possible.

Chapter Six Exercises

STAKES EXERCISE

Watch an episode of a reality program where stakes are especially important. Pay close attention to any moments that seem to be especially driven by interview and host voice over. Ask yourself if you believe that these stakes were evident at the time the content was shot, or added in post. If you believe that the entire scene was repurposed, move on to the next exercise.

STAKES EXERCISE 2: REPURPOSED SCENE EXERCISE

Take note of a more benign scene that moves story forward, but doesn't seem explosive or revelatory. Now, figure out how you would make that scene seem as if the participants interacting are at odds, becoming friends, or hiding something from each other.

What interview pickups would you need in order to make this scene about something else? Based on interview content seen in the rest of the episode, would it be in keeping with the true character of the cast members?

NOTES PASS EXERCISE ONE

Watch an episode of a reality show as if you were an EP or network exec, writing up your notes on how the episode could be improved. Once you've finished your notes, set them aside for an hour and then read them, answering the following questions on each note:

- On a scale of one to ten, how easily interpreted is your note?
- On a scale of one to ten, how difficult do you expect it would be to address this note? In other words, would it involve reshoots or additional time with voiceover or host talent?
- Is your tone constructive or derogatory? How would you feel if you received this note?

NOTES PASS EXERCISE TWO

Watch a second reality show, preferably a prime-time cable docusoap. Imagine that your role is that of the network executive once again, but that you've just received a mandate that shows on the network need to be "toned down" to contain less overtly sexual or verbally offensive material.

Give notes that could actually be addressed, using resources likely to be available already. Some suggestions might include: removing or bleeping some dialogue, removing some scene content, or asking if alternate coverage may be available.

Editor Billy DiCicco works on an episode of a reality series at Shed Media in Burbank. (photo by the author)

Get to Work!

By now, you know most of what goes on behind the scenes of your favorite reality shows. Now all that remains for those of you ready to take on the business is finding out how to get your foot in the door.

Virtually no one starts out as a Story Producer. In the entire course of my career, I've only seen it happen once, when an Executive Producer hired an old college friend of his for that position. By mid-season, his pal was out the door and the rest of the story team was racing to pick up her slack.

We all start at the bottom and should, because there's a huge learning curve when it comes to understanding the process well enough to tell great stories. Hang in there, because if you play your cards right, this stage of your career won't last long.

Entry-Level Positions

I've seen receptionists and executive assistants become Story Producers, and even a few Editors I know have taken mid-career stabs at straight-up story gigs. By and large, however, most story folks come up through a few key positions.

Remember those Loggers and Transcribers I mentioned back in Chapter Three? You can't beat those jobs for gaining experience while enjoying daily access to your potential mentors in the story department.

In major entertainment cities, job listings for Loggers and Transcribers abound in the pages of websites like *www.craigslist.org*, *www.mandy.com*, *www.entertainmentcareers.net*, and *www.realitystaff.com*. Cold-calling Post Supervisors at reality production companies can also work; most of them prefer to work with experienced people, but don't let that keep you from applying. Never send a blind fax, as they're seldom read.

> "In this business, everything is word-of-mouth. You build up a reputation that carries you through day after day, year after year."
>
> **—HECTOR RAMIREZ,** Camera Operator and most nominated individual in the history of the Emmy Awards[1]

1 "Emmy's Most Nominated Individual Adds Five," *Hollywood Reporter*, July 8, 2010.

When you're called in to interview, be sure to ask about which software the company uses to log tapes. There are many kinds (like PilotWare and Teresis, for example) and knowing enough to ask implies that you have at least a passing familiarity with the business. Be candid if you're unfamiliar with a program they mention — most are easy to learn, but impossible to bluff any competency with once you show up to work.

Once you're hired, always take the day shift if you're given the choice. You'll have many more opportunities to interact with the higher-ups if you're in the office while everyone else is there. My first logging job was a 7 p.m. to 3 a.m. shift, but I always dropped by the office around 5 p.m. to check in and nab some "face time" with everyone before the daytime crowd bailed out at 6 or 7.

There are two ways to approach logging and transcribing:

One, come in every day ten minutes late and looking like you dressed yourself out of your glove box, log half your tapes, take an hour and eighteen minutes for lunch, log your other tapes, and head home complaining about how everyone on the show is an overpaid pain in the butt who doesn't notice you until they're breathing down your neck about typos.

TIP When inquiring about Logger or Transcriber positions, know your typing speed in case you're asked . . . there are plenty of free tests online to help you determine it.

Two, come in every day ten minutes early and dressed like someone with a job, drop by the story department to ask if there's anything they need you to keep an eye out for, log half your tapes, spend your lunch break relaxing but thinking about what you've been reviewing, and generally seize every opportunity to prove yourself as something more than a despondent robot wage-slave. Finish the day by asking the story folks if anyone needs anything else before you head home.

If you can manage the second approach without overdoing it, you'll likely get some solid references out of your Post Supervisor and the story people you've worked with. You may also find yourself in the story department next season as a Story Assistant or alternately titled Assistant Story Producer.

Asking for opportunities and making your long-term goals clear is crucial. I've known Loggers and Transcribers who have worked in the same positions for years, and plenty of others (like me) who were able to turn their work ethic and story sense into story positions in just a few months to a year because we made it known that we wanted to learn and move up the creative ladder.

If it doesn't happen for you on the first show, just lather, rinse, and repeat. Your day will come.

> "As I've built up my experience and moved forward, I continued to work under the same title of Story Producer but take on additional responsibilities. At some point most of us find ourselves in a classic catch-22. Companies are happy to have you do the work, especially when you're good, but reluctant to give a higher title whether deserved or not. You can't move up to a better position (Supervising Story Producer, Supervising Producer . . .) without the title on your resume but how do you get the title when no one will move you up?"
>
> — **HEATHER J. MILLER,** Supervising Story Producer

Now . . . if logging and transcribing isn't your cup of tea, you can try landing a job as a Production Assistant, either in the office or in the field.

Production Assistant work is also an attractive option because employment opportunities aren't unique to major entertainment cities. Reality shows travel everywhere, and local-hire gigs ranging from a few days to several weeks are rare but findable on your local version of Craigslist.

As a "PA" in the field, you'll get to see Field Producers (and sometimes Story Producers) in action. In the office, you'll have regular chances to ask questions and express your interest in eventually working in story to your Supervising Producers, Line Producers, and other folks.

While your job will feel completely removed from writing (picking up sandwiches or unloading equipment requires little story sense), remember the actual point — you are inside production and building the relationships that will eventually pay off with an opportunity.

Whether you break in as a Logger, Transcriber, or Production Assistant, what's important is that you get in the door, listen, learn, and start making contacts.

The Story Department

Congratulations. You've graduated from your entry-level position and are now a Story Assist. Bring on the glamour!

I kid, of course.

Story Assistants primarily aid Story Producers in hunting down sound bites and requested bits of source material. It's not exactly exciting stuff, and the real reason you're chasing these content fragments is because it's not cost-effective to have a Story Producer making two or three times your rate waste their time on it. Be prepared to spend several hours one day combing source tapes and logs for a shot of a celebrity feeding his fish and the rest of the day trying to find someone else saying the word "pumpkin."

Before you decide to throw yourself from the nearest window, remember that this is just another rung on the ladder that provides innumerable opportunities to show off your story skills. Your next step to story producing is easy: Earn the respect of your story staff to a point where you're asked to do scene work.[1]

This will usually happen once post is well under way and the show starts to bump up against deadlines. As you notice your story staff shifting in tone from cheery let's-go-for-lunch camaraderie to a state of weeping and gnashing of teeth, spring into action and ask if you can be of assistance with any scene work. After all, you're clearly familiar with the show, and what's the harm in throwing some light bit of business your way?

Other chances to flex your creative muscles include composing teases (the content that typically runs at the end of the first act to hook the viewer on exciting content to come), writing or rewriting voiceover content, and handling promotional selects and bonus scene requests from the network (show highlights and mini-scenes that can be used online to promote the show, respectively).

Do these things well, and with a bit of luck, next season you'll be a full-on Story Producer.

Bad news. No glamour there either. But it's a lot more fun.

---

1 As with all things, it may come along faster if you ask for it.

"When Troy offered me my first job as a Story Assistant for his show, I had at that point only worked in other kinds of television production in the past, and I had absolutely no experience in or familiarity with working in reality television. But Troy reassured me that it would be very easy to pick up and that I'd be working with a great bunch of people. Turned out he was right on both counts. I really enjoy working as a Story Assistant, since working so closely with the Story Producers, assisting them in whatever capacity they needed, and watching how they did things also helped me to learn just how the whole process of putting together a reality TV show in postproduction works."

—KAREN SNYDER, Story Assistant, *Basketball Wives*

The Politics of Reality

What makes reality television tough to handle for the Story Producers who toil behind the scenes is the fact that many believe that the illusion of reality, the imitation of life you're creating for millions of viewers, depends on complete denial of the process. It's kind of the same deal as hot dogs — the makers assume that the less consumers really know about how the product comes together, the better.

Some reality-driven cable networks have gone so far as to brand themselves with slogans like "Life Unscripted" and "Not Reality — Actuality." Thank heaven they can turn on a few cameras for thirty minutes to an hour and walk away with a show, eh?

A few words of advice guaranteed to preserve your sanity — get over the need for public acknowledgment. But just before you do that, consider joining the WGA's Nonfiction Writers Caucus. You can learn more about their efforts to gain recognition (as well as health and pension benefits) for reality show writers at *www.wga.org*.

"That Stuff Has Writers?" — Building a Reputation on an Invisible Job

The best story producing creates results that appear seamless, so when your uncle seems surprised that his favorite reality program, yours, has writers, take it as a compliment.

Promoting yourself within the confines of the reality production universe is far more important than seeking public recognition for your hard work. Remember where those checks come from.

To that end, I've worked hard to build a reputation among my peers that's predicated on a few basic principles:

- Be fun to work with.
- Tell the best story possible *under the conditions you've been hired to work in*.
- Edify the people you work with and help them to advance.

Notice the italics above? Telling the best story possible under the conditions I've been hired to work in means giving it my all without killing myself on productions with problematic network execs, poor quality source material, or any of the other roadblocks that can crop up. Remember the phrase that can save your sanity when everything's going south: "It's just television."

Dan O'Shannon, a writer and Executive Producer for *Frasier* and *Modern Family*, once advised: "As you're coming up through the ranks, remember that your job is not to make the best TV you can but to make your Executive Producer happy. Sometimes these two goals are worlds apart."[2] While that's some sage advice no matter what genre you're in, sometimes your Executive Producer or someone at the network will give you a note that can't be addressed due to lack of source material or wishful thinking. When, after making best efforts to comply, you don't have the content to make an interviewee "sound more excited" or create something that didn't happen out of whole cloth, just acknowledge the issue, document your attempt to address the note (because they'll ask if you tried), and move on.

Good execs recognize hard work, so there's no reason to panic. Keep doing your best and that will be enough to build a reputation on.

Ethics

There are a lot of nasty, mean-spirited shows out there, and depending on the kind of person you are, working on them can really grind you down. Cast members will sign away everything just to be on television, up to and including the right to be portrayed accurately. While one can argue that

---

2 As quoted in Writing for Episodic Television: http://www.wga.org/uploadedFiles/writers_resources/ep_quotes.pdf

anyone desperate enough to take a stab at reality stardom gets what they deserve, I think most of them just don't have any idea how sharp the teeth on the machine can be until it's far too late.

I've learned the hard way to avoid shows that trade on negativity and humiliation, always putting myself in the position of the participant. How would I feel if something I said was intentionally taken out of context? What would I have to explain to my family and friends as an embarrassing fabrication? How would I feel if a guy in a seven-foot monster costume jumped out of my closet and scared me?

A few true items from the trenches:

- A woman who might not have passed a psychological exam (now pretty much an industry standard during casting) was allowed to appear on a top talent competition program. After being humiliated on national television, she committed suicide in front of one of the judges' homes.[3]
- An unwitting couple vacationing in Las Vegas returned to their hotel room to find what they believed was a dead body. They were detained by actors posing as security guards while police and EMS workers were summoned. Only later were they informed that they were being featured on a prank series.[4]
- An unwitting participant on a different prank series sued for severe emotional and physical trauma after her experience on the show. While she was riding in a car that she thought was bound for a Hollywood event, the radio malfunctioned before announcing that the United States had been taken over by aliens. She ran from the vehicle and was confronted by an actor in full alien getup, believing she was about to be killed.[5]

Carefully consider the spirit of the shows you're offered. Can you live with working on these kinds of programs for most of your waking hours and months at a time?

This brings me to another important point.

---

3 *www.TheWrap.com*, June 1, 2009: "The Wrap Investigates: 11 Players Have Committed Suicide."
4 *www.BroadcastingCable.com*, February 13, 2005, "A Reality Waiting to Happen."
5 Ibid.

Saying No: Building the Resume You Want

Many years ago, long before reality television and I were acquainted, I attended a seminar in which Michael Wiese, publisher of this very book, shared a lesson he'd learned about how saying "no" to less than ideal opportunities freed him up to say "yes" to better ones when they came along.

When I'm offered a show that's far below my rate, mean-spirited, or just plain dopey, I have no problem saying "no." The television universe is a big place. Better shows are out there waiting to be made, and old friends and associates may be just days or even hours away from calling to offer me a chance to work with them again.

Try not to look at jobs from a standpoint of desperation and scarcity, as if that lowball offer on a zero-budget series about an abusive, drug-addled Z-list star will be the last offer you ever get. Remember, you and your friends will know you worked on that piece of junk unless you keep it mum and omit it from your resume. Even so, the credit might pop up to haunt you on *www.imdb.com* or similar sites.

Now why would you give months of your life to an utterly valueless credit you're ashamed of? Yes, I already know — it's a paycheck. But so is the better show you had to say "no" to because you'd already accepted employment on the crummy show.

So what kind of credits should you say "yes" to in order to boost your perceived value to employers?

Major broadcast network credits tend to carry more weight than basic cable shows, primarily because network shows are so heavily promoted (read: easily recognizable) and typically higher-rated (read: successful). A few of those dotting your resume will give you the look of a heavy hitter who won't leap at lower offers.

That said, innovative cable shows that excite you are always worth taking, especially personality-driven material that will enable you to show off your skills as a storyteller instead of a simple time-cruncher.

None of us can predict which shows will be hits, but it's not hard to guess which shows will make your resume look ridiculous and kick your self-esteem in the teeth. Avoid them and be happy!

Never be afraid to say "no" when your enjoyment of your job or the integrity of your resume is at stake.

Advancing Your Career

One of the major obstacles to advancement in reality television is that almost everyone in a position to hire you will go to friends and previous associates first when staffing a story department. As the years go by, here's some advice on making sure past coworkers and employers think of you first.

Keep track of your past coworkers by maintaining a database (or at least a hard-copy file) of their contact info, handily provided for you on each production in the form of call sheets. If you see a familiar name scroll by at the end of something you're watching, drop them an email or social network message to let them know you saw and enjoyed their latest effort. Between shows, try to meet up for lunch with your old colleagues once in a while. What you're doing is maintaining your garden of references and potential job leads without being the jerk no one hears from until they get cc'd on an email blast begging for work.

Beyond that, there are other ways to cast a wider net and boost your contact count.

Networking in the Reality Community

Opportunities for working reality professionals to network proliferate in open, closed, or even secret Facebook groups bearing names like "I Need an Editor," "I Need a Producer," and more. These primarily function as employment listings,[6] but can also remind you of people you've worked with but may have forgotten about.

Professional networking site LinkedIn (*www.linkedin.com*) features a group titled "Alternative and Reality Television Professionals." Once your career is up and running, LinkedIn's structure will help you to connect with other pros by requesting introductions from your existing mutual contacts. A word of advice for this site, as with all other networking done online or off: Never recommend someone you don't know or whose work you can't vouch for. Preserve the value of your recommendations so that when you need to help someone you believe in, your word will carry weight.

---

6 Be careful not to violate protocol in these groups or you'll be tossed out.

Networking in the Broader Television Community

If you studied media at a college or university with a well-established alumni program, failing to take advantage of those alumni connections is positively criminal. In Los Angeles, alumni organizations from UCLA, USC, Tisch, Ithaca, Syracuse, and many others host regular events for their graduates. Heck, if you graduated from Harvard, you can't throw a rock without hitting a job lead in Los Angeles.

If your college doesn't have an alumni presence where you live and work, get the ball rolling yourself. I started Full Sail University's West Coast Alumni organization in 2001, and through the efforts of our graduates on message boards and at our infrequent gatherings, the job leads keep flying. [7]

In Los Angeles, New York, and other major entertainment cities, watch for seminars and panels that are open to the public. For one-on-one networking, my favorites here in Los Angeles are those put on by the Caucus for Producers, Writers & Directors (*www.caucus.org*). Panels include industry heavyweights of all stripes, and pay attention, because so do the tables that surround you.

Professional Organizations

Joining the LA-based Academy of Television Arts and Sciences (*www.emmys.org*) gives you access to their members-only events, which are great for meeting other professionals not only in reality TV, but across ATAS's full peer group spectrum. As a member of the Nonfiction Peer Group, you'll also be able to attend members-only seminars and panels that offer access to top reality professionals and network execs. I strongly recommend ATAS's student membership to anyone studying film or television at an accredited institution, as adding professional affiliations to your resume early on can paint you as a serious-minded individual to prospective employers even before you've built solid working credits.

If you don't live in Los Angeles, never fear! Across the country, the National Academy of Television Arts and Sciences boasts (as of this writing) some nineteen chapters. You can find them at *www.emmyonline.org* and yes, they have student memberships as well.

---

7 Full Sail University does an amazing job of keeping alumni connected on their own in cities across the country. Be sure to take advantage of your own college/university connections.

The Producers Guild of America, online at *www.producersguild.org*, hosts many events each year and will consider (on an individual basis) Field Producers, Segment Producers, and Story Producers for membership based on experience and actual job function.

The Hollywood Radio & Television Society is an organization of execs representing broadcast and cable networks, studios, talent and management agencies, producers, legal and financial firms, new media companies, and more to address issues that are relevant to the ongoing success and future of our business. Their ticketed events feature some of the most powerful folks in the industry, and are great for networking. You can find more about them and their events at *www.hrts.org*.

The Caucus for Producers, Writers & Directors (again, at *www.caucus.org*) was originally formed over thirty years ago with the stated goals of elevating the quality and diversity of television and restoring creative rights to the members of the creative community at large. They continue to evolve as both an honor society and a source of mentorship to new creative talents. While it's an organization for mid-career and fully matured professionals, their industry panels and events are open to the public at nominal cost.

Maximizing IMDb and Other Resume and Credit Websites

As you network, be sure that you are visible on important resume and credit websites that are referenced later by those professionals you've just met as they seek to verify just who you really are.

The Internet Movie Database or IMDb (located at *www.imdb.com*) is a website chock-full of compiled cast and crew credits for movies and television shows. Many, if not most, employers will cross-check your resume against credits listed there, also seeking out potential hires by pulling up a successful show in the same vein as their new project and scoping out the folks who made it happen.

While it's unlikely that Brad Pitt or Julia Roberts have much to worry about in the way of having any credits go unlisted there, you should make yourself responsible for ensuring that you are not only listed on IMDb, but that the credits listed there for you are accurate.

You can submit revisions and credits yourself, but don't volunteer an abundance of personal information in your listing. I'm still trying to get over having had my birthday (including the year) submitted to my profile by someone.

If you can swing it, subscribe to their Pro service at *www.imdbpro.com* so that you can reap the added benefit of being able to pull up contact information for producers and production companies when it comes time for you to go hunting for work.

In addition to adding your data to IMDb, you'll also want to make sure you keep your resume updated at *http://staffmeup.com*. The website, founded originally as realitystaff.com by Jared Tobman, Managing Partner and Co-Founder of Trium Entertainment, has established itself as one of the top sites for experienced professionals in the genre to connect with future employers and employees alike.

Another frequently used site for referencing credits is *www.inbaseline.com*, which is updated regularly by a full-time research staff.

Some Thoughts on Networking

Let me close out this chapter with this bit of advice: Network like crazy, but with sincerity. No one likes to feel used, and it's more important to build relationships than to hand out your business cards in bulk. Take both the time to learn from those who came before you and to pass what you've learned on to the newbies who follow.

And now, on to the chapter I've teased you about long enough — the one where I tell you how to make a million dollars off an idea you wrote down on a napkin.

Or, rather, not.

Chapter Seven Exercises

THE ETHICS GUT-CHECK

Answer the following questions truthfully, explaining why at the end of each answer.

- Could you work on a prank show where unsuspecting targets are subjected to funny situations? Why?
- Could you work on a prank show where those targets are frightened instead of simply put in funny situations? Why?
- Could you work on a show where the drama is mostly negative/exploitive? Why?

NETWORKING: JOIN SOMETHING!

If you are a student, find and join a professional organization like ATAS at the student level. Are there any local film organizations or groups that you can join? If not, consider seeking out an online community.

If you are no longer in school and not yet working in your desired professional field, consider joining any local organization with regular meetings just to brush up on your conversational skills.

If you are already a working media professional or educator in the media arts, find an organization that you can join at an academic level. ATAS offers this.

NETWORKING: ASK A QUESTION!

Watch a favorite reality show and single out a Supervising Story Producer or Story Producer whose name appears in the credits of an episode you enjoyed. If you can find them online or by dropping them a line at their production company, ask them a few questions about their process and what advice they'd give to someone looking for a career in reality television.

Don't be shy. And don't ask me in this exercise, because I'm the easy target. Make a connection!

The imposing 10 Universal City Plaza Building, also known as the "Black Tower" to Hollywood insiders, plays home to NBC/Comcast and many of their subsidiary networks.
(photo by the author)

Creating Your Own Shows

"A lot of the 'reality TV advice' that litters the Internet was written by people who've never sold or made a show, or don't understand how the unscripted television business works."

— **JOKE FINCIOEN AND BIAGIO MESSINA,** Joke Productions /
www.producingunscripted.com

L et me take a moment to say hello to all the get-rich-quick types who went directly to this chapter as they browsed in the bookstore: Hi, folks. Buy this book and start at the beginning.

Most people think pitching a reality show is as easy as coming up with an idea, and that after walking into meetings for a few weeks repeating "it's about a family that runs a junkyard" or "ten people live in a house and have to decide which of them is hottest," that someone will cut them a check and they can spend the rest of their lives living it up in Malibu.

Not so. At least, not usually.

Creating a reality series and gaining access to people who can make it happen is a rough go for someone new to the genre, though nothing's impossible.

Before You Begin: Understanding the Market

Whenever I hear anybody say that they want to set out to redefine something, or that they think their projects are more creative and innovative than anything else on television, my arm goes numb. They will sometimes go on to tell me how a reality show about a bunch of treehouse-building vampires who also run a sex-toy business is edgier than anything currently on television, announcing how they fully expect that execs will be blown away by the pitch, which will be like nothing television has ever seen.[1]

First rule: *Know what the networks are buying.*

What network do you know that seems like the perfect home for a show about treehouse-building vampires who sell sex toys?

Go ahead. I'll give you a minute.

Can't think of one? Exactly. I doubt that HGTV is waiting by the phone to set that meeting.

Networks are in a constant state of flux as far as what it is they want to see. You can't necessarily determine their taste by watching what's currently on the air, but if you pay attention to what they're buying *as they're buying it*, you'll be in better shape. You can do this by simply keeping up with announcements in the online trades like *Variety* and the *Hollywood Reporter*.[2]

The Workable Concept

Now, let's put your new show through its second test. Ask yourself this: Can it realistically be made?

Let's say you came up with a show called *Celebrity Choir*, featuring twenty new celebrities every week coming together to form a choir. You'd really need to ask yourself if the show could even *find* 160 willing celebrities to participate in an eight-episode season. Further reflection on the probable cost and nightmare logistics of even getting all twenty celebrities to the set quickly transforms *Celebrity Choir* from a cool concept into a total turkey.

Once you land on a realistic, exciting, workable format, it's time to start thinking about your pitch.

---

1 This is the part where I lose all sensation in my face, complementing the arm numbness.

2 If HGTV suddenly starts buying shows about renovating sexy haunted houses, I take back what I said about your treehouse-building-vampires-who-sell-sex-toys show.

The Pitch

As with all film or television concepts bracing for market, you'll need a solid pitch . . . a brief distillation of what your show is about that can be verbally related to a prospective production partner or network exec in just a few minutes.

Rumor has it that the 1987 film *Dragnet* had the shortest pitch of all time, just a bar of the original TV show's theme song followed by the name of the star: "Dunnnn da dun dun . . . Dan Aykroyd." While it's unlikely that your show will boil down into something quite that simple, it's important you hook the listener just as quickly with the first line or two of your pitch.

I always kick mine off with a question (for example: "What would happen if six college students from New York City suddenly found themselves broke in Tokyo?") or some variation of the show's logline, the single-sentence description of the show that conveys the basic idea as well as where your conflict will come from.[3]

Some logline examples from my own files:

- "Eight cast members spend a season touring allegedly haunted locations, challenged each week to tell the difference between tall tales and terrifying true stories with the ultimate goal of winning a cash prize."
- "Can legendary songwriter, artist, technologist, and Hollywood party thrower Allee Willis continue her self-guided, self-funded artistic evolution without losing her eye-popping home base, the kitschy palace of creativity known as Willis Wonderland?"
- "We've seen the beautiful people fall in love on TV for years . . . now it's time for the geeks to make a few love connections."

Once you've got your show boiled down into a simple logline, flesh out the rest of your pitch. Keep it short. Two or three minutes, tops. Worried that that's not enough time to explain every facet of your show? Don't be. A well-done, exciting two- or three-minute pitch can turn into a half-hour meeting on the spot if you manage to get the listener excited about an idea.

---

3 Loglines serve a number of purposes, most importantly kick-starting the imagination of anyone who reads them. Think of them as the calling cards for your project.

For now, though, just concentrate on how you can describe your show to a potential buyer in just a minute or two.

As with the logline, the object is to tease the buyer into wanting to know more, not to just vomit information. Think about your last encounter with a salesperson who had memorized every detail of the product they were selling, soullessly barfing product specs and catchphrases. Your pitch is supposed to engage, not repel . . . build in opportunities for your pitchee to participate or respond when you can!

Remember, the sooner you wrap up your pitch, the sooner the exec can start asking questions. It's also a good idea to go into every meeting with at least two backup ideas in case things go sideways and the exec says, "Not interested, but what else have you got?"

Don't be discouraged if a show doesn't sell itself in the room. That's a rarity, even when the show is of interest to the exec you're pitching it to. Chances are, the person you're meeting with answers to someone else, and they'll need to kick your show upstairs for further discussion.

> "Whatever makes the buyer want to buy it is what makes a pitch rock: whether it's the originality of the idea, the talent, the cast, or just good timing. You know when a pitch sucks: It's when you can't wait to get out of the room."
>
> **—NICK EMMERSON**, Managing Director, Warner Bros. Television Productions UK

And that's why you need something called a "one-sheet."

The One-Sheet

The basic contents of your pitch should be memorialized in a one-sheet.[4] Here's an example of how I do mine:

---

4 Sometimes also referred to as a "leave behind," as at the end of the meeting, if there's any interest, you may be asked if you have anything to "leave behind."

ARTHOUSE

If your walls could talk . . . what could they say about your style?

LOGLINE

Humdrum rooms are enlivened by makeovers inspired by a single piece of art added to the space.

THE SHOW

When the average homeowner thinks about adding original works of art to their home, dollar signs start swimming in their heads. *ArtHouse*, with the help of our art- and design-savvy host, will unite homeowners each week with a local artist, help select a piece for the home, and turn the room it's displayed in into a thematic showplace.

STRUCTURE

Each episode begins with our host dropping in to assess our guest family's personal style. From there, we'll bring in a local artist who'll present three works for the family to choose from.

Now that the artwork's been selected, it's time to incorporate it into the home. A wild pop-art painting of a pirate might inspire an all-out pirate-themed room, while an abstract work in calming blues and greens might inspire a restful sanctuary. Just as every work of art is different, so will be the makeovers they inspire. New color schemes, furniture selections, specialty lighting, and more will provide viewers with the inspiration they need to add some artistic flavor to their own homes!

No makeover show is complete without a proper reveal to friends and neighbors, so we'll end each episode with a small gathering of acquaintances to ooh and aah over our homeowners' new rooms.

It's easier to bring real art home than you think!

Simple, simple, simple. So simple, it's tough for an exec to pick apart — the more details you provide in a one-sheet, the less opportunity a potential buyer or production company has to fill in the blanks on their own. You wouldn't think that's a bad thing, but in this day and age, it can be.

I pitched a show to the Director of Development at a major cable network, the meeting ending with an enthusiastic proclamation that the show was "the best thing that ever came across [his] desk." He could hardly wait to present it to his boss, sure it was a slam-dunk. The one-sheet I left behind had an odd image incorporated into it that led to the immediate dismissal of the show as "too dark" for the network *without even reading the material*. Would the big boss have been as interested in the show if I'd left that one piece of information (the photo) out of the leave-behind? Maybe. He certainly would have been left to his own imagination in interpreting what we'd presented.

There's a downside to being *too* vague as well. I recently pitched to a production company that so jumped the gun and second-guessed the show from having read the logline alone that when it didn't match their preconceived (yet unexpressed) idea of what the show was about, it brought our meeting to a screeching halt.[5]

The only time you need more information in a one-sheet would be in the case of a competition/elimination reality show or series, in which case you'll need to explain the basics of game play and the metric by which players are eliminated, but in no more detail than this:

> *"Two homeowners will be given works of art by the same artist, then compete to see which of their art-inspired room makeovers will win the hearts and votes of three local designers we invite to judge."*

Some special advice specific to reality-competition/elimination pitches and one-sheets: *Keep the rules of game play simple.* If Joe Viewer can't follow along and understand how your show works, he's going to flip that channel — and the execs know it.

Mark Burnett, the man behind the popular *Survivor* franchise and other hits, once created a show called *Pirate Master* in which he loaded

---

5 Unless you've already had a string of giant successes, don't pull the *auteur* card.

a pirate ship with a bunch of contestants in search of treasure in a sort of *"Survivor* at sea." It was a tasty premise in the wake of the first two *Pirates of the Caribbean* films, which had already raked in hundreds of millions at the box office.

On *Pirate Master*, contestants vied for booty in various challenges, which they could then use to strike deals with one another or try to ensure their long-term security in other ways. The booty also had an actual value, so trading it away was like spending your winnings. Cast members up for elimination were marked with a "black spot," and players who were eliminated each week were "cut adrift." In the end, whoever found the largest stash of booty offered on the show would win $500,000.

The show, some speculate, ultimately sank under the weight of its complex game play. It was yanked from the CBS schedule before the end of its debut season, the final episodes appearing only online.[6]

Now, while I've just told you that your in-the-room pitch should be kept short, simple, and a bit generalized, it doesn't mean that you shouldn't know everything there is to know about your show before you walk into a room. If the execs are engaged, there will be lots of questions like these:

"What happens in the event of a tie?"
"How do you see this playing out over a full season?"
"Is there an Internet component?"

Holy smoke! You didn't write all *that* down on the back of the million-dollar napkin when you dreamed this up, did you?

Have your answers ready. Draft a friend to bounce your pitch off of who can then ask you every tough question they can conjure up. Brace yourself for battle! The more complete your vision, the readier you'll be to help spin it into existence in the minds of those who can make it happen.

Bolster your pitch with a treatment of three to five pages explaining the ins and outs of your show including detailed game play, rules, a season's worth of episode ideas, a breakdown of a sample episode, and/ or whatever best illustrates your point and expands your idea into an

---

6 Even the greats like Burnett have a misfire once in a while. A so-called "failure" that makes it to air and puts a check in your pocket is still, by my definition, a success.

understandable whole. Don't offer the treatment unless you're asked for it, but have it ready.

The Deck

Before we launch into discussing whether or not you should consider adding a video component to your pitch/presentation, let's talk about decks for a moment. A "deck" is a presentation comprised of several pages (or slides, if you'd doing them in the time-honored PowerPoint format) that allows you to share a concept, introducing cast and details of play or production, spelling out the vision of the show in a static visual format.

Admittedly, animations and video can be embedded in a deck, but ultimately, what you want is something visual that can be printed off for review and passed around in hard copy if necessary.

While there is no standardized format that a deck should be composed in, I strongly suggest, at a bare minimum, that your deck have separate pages outlining the following:

- Show title graphic
- Logline
- Description of the series (single page or slide)
- If applicable, core and supporting cast mini bios and photos
- If applicable, description of game play / list of games

The Sizzle Reel

If a deck isn't enough to get your idea across, and seeing your cast or concept in action seems the only way to go, consider making a "sizzle reel," a produced video that conveys the concept for your show. More often now than ever before, execs expect to see tape (video in DVD format, actually . . . the word "tape" is a quaint holdover from the days of VHS) for proof of concept.[7]

Sizzle reels can be a short as a promo (a fake "commercial" teasing your show) or as elaborate as a sample scene or two. According to producer Daniel Lawrence Abrams,[8] there are a number of different kinds of sizzles you can make:

---

7 Evidence that your show will work.
8 Daniel Lawrence Abrams, "Sizzle Reels: Produce Before You Pitch," producersguild.org/?sizzle

"Rip-o-matic"
Exclusively cut from existing footage from other sources.
(Technically illegal and may expose you to civil liability) (Duration:
one to seven minutes)

"Talent Sizzle"
This kind of tape focuses exclusively on the talent/subjects, often
in their natural environment, interacting with people as they
usually do coupled with soundbites from sit-down interviews.
(Duration: one to five minutes)

"Teaser Sizzle"
An exciting promo that does not explicitly outline the elements
of the show or specifically how it works. (Duration: one to two
minutes)

"Standard Sizzle"
An extended promo like a movie trailer which showcases the
talent/subjects involved, an overview of the show, and gives a
specific sense of the creative direction/vision. (Duration: two to
seven minutes)

"Presentation Tape"
A bit like the standard sizzle but likely also with full scenes if not
full segments/acts to present how the show will actually look to the
TV audience. (Duration: seven to twenty minutes)

"Independent Pilot"
A full version of the show as it would be seen by the TV audience.
These function like network-commissioned "non-airing pilots"
which are done at a substantial discount to full pilots that are
intended to air.

No matter which route you go, with just a good quality camera and
Final Cut Pro, it's easier to produce sizzles now than ever before.

My personal preference? Keep sizzle reels brief. Typically three minutes or less. Many of my own are about half that. *Don't give an exec time
to grow bored or they'll turn on you.*

Rumor has it that *The Osbournes* was sold based on some old *MTV
Cribs*-like footage of a walkthrough of one of Ozzy's homes shot in the
early '90s. Ozzy's teenage offspring Jack and Kelly were but wee Ozzy

pups in the material, but the basic idea, music's "Prince of Darkness" as family man, shone through. The sizzle neatly conveyed an image of Ozzy at home that was vastly different than the onstage wild man that his fans had enjoyed for decades. A doting wife? Two funny kids? Who knew?

Decide what's most important to get across when you're scripting your sizzle. If you're building a show around a celebrity, fame alone isn't enough — you need to convey what makes them special and what their stories and struggles are. If you're pitching a dating show, you'd better be ready to show the powers that be what makes it different than the other ones already on air. As supplementary material supporting your pitch, the sizzle reel is your best weapon in selling a buyer on the unique nature of your show.

Here's the loose script for a sizzle reel I worked on with Ric Viers, author of *The Sound Effects Bible* and *The Location Sound Bible*, for *Wild Tracks*, a show about his crazy professional adventures. As you read it, you'll see what we felt was important in setting him up as an interesting, if not exactly "famous at a household level," subject:

I'm Ric Viers, and whether you've heard of me or not . . .

(smashing car window, etc.)

I can guarantee you've heard my work.

(montage of major movie sound effects in action)

I'm one of the world's biggest and busiest sound effects producers . . . and with my team at the Detroit Chop Shop . . .

(see the team)

There's virtually nothing I can't make sound awesome.

(Comedy "before" shot sans sound, quick shot of Ric creating the sound to be used, then "after" shot of same thing with sound, Ric giving it the thumbs-up)

I've got the best team on Earth . . .

(Funny/klutzy/goofy soundup of Ric and team getting into it . . . lower thirds)

. . . the respect of my family . . .

(Zingy/cut interaction with wife 'n' kiddo in work environment)

. . . and this thing.

(Weird object that creates an unexpected sound)

(Montage of family/work interaction, crazy action)

(LOGO: Ric Viers' WILD TRACKS)

Sounds good, right?

While we ended up adding to it a bit, this basic concept conveyed Ric's on-camera charm, his place in the industry, and the notion that the world of sound effects can be entertaining. Sure, the one-sheet says the same thing, but it's a lot more fun watching Ric scrape swords together in his studio or a montage of incredible film clips featuring his effects in action in major films, shows, and videogames.

"I'm a walking reality show. Always have been and always will be. I've shot every significant moment of my life since 1978. But because I don't like to be the second person to do anything, the only way that I would do a reality show the way things are today with nine thousand other people doing them would be if mine was quantumly different."

—**ALLEE WILLIS**, Songwriter, Artist, Technologist, and Party Thrower

With *Launching Allee*, songwriter, artist, technologist, and Hollywood party thrower Allee Willis and I undertook a far more complex production that not only related who she was and that she was entertaining, but also conveyed her fascination with process, the wonderfully out-there hook for the show being her day-to-day involvement in the making of her own show. Allee oversaw every creative detail of the promo, slaving over the effects and animations that brought it to life, imbuing it with her own inimitable style. The amount of work that went into that promo as opposed to any others I'd done to date was staggering . . . but you couldn't deny that it was positively arresting. I may be as fond of that sizzle reel as I am of any finished program I've ever worked on . . . it's a great character study and concept piece all in one.

Whether your sizzle reel is as mind-bending as the one for *Launching Allee* or as simple as sharing an old clip of the Osbournes at home, all it has to do is the one thing it must not fail to do: Make people understand what you're selling in an entertaining way. If anyone in the room is left thinking "I don't get it," you're back to square one. Square zero, actually.

Worried that you don't have much of a budget to produce your sizzle reel? Never fear. A sizzle reel isn't for show or sale, so there's little need to sweat clearance issues for music and borrowed images. It's there to convey your concept to a couple of folks in a room. If I were pitching a series about tough-guy bikers who throw tea parties for kids, I might borrow a well-known rock track and some classical music to help push the idea over the top on the sizzle. If you get lucky and the show goes to series, yes, that rock anthem or orchestra piece is going to have to be paid for. But for a sizzle reel, forget it.

Now here's an odd turn. Say you're in the room pitching a reality show that you've been knocking around in your head for years. The exec has just heard your pitch, watched your sizzle reel, and is now folding his hands into the legendary "I'm thinking" triangular prayer position just under his chin. You can see your show getting sold. You've mentally wrapped your hands around the steering wheel of your new Mercedes.[9] The exec seems to vanish into outer space for just a moment, then looks you deep in the eyes and says, "Could this be a game show?" It's an interesting and terrifying question, because the show you just pitched is about the lives of a group of animal handlers at the local zoo.

You've got two options here. Explain to the exec that no, this isn't a game show, it's a reality series, or roll with it and ask how he sees the game show working. It's your call. Should you shut down the exec's seemingly nutty idea or let the conversation roll?

I can think of at least one real-life instance where the result of letting the exec free-associate and fiddle around with a pitch resulted in the sale of a show that birthed a spin-off brand empire for the creators who brought it in. You'd know the show. You'd probably even know the producers. Scenarios like this happen *all the time* in reality TV.

> "One of the most important concepts to remember when pitching an original show idea is to bring a collaborative spirit into the meeting room. The making of a successful project comes through sharing experiences, partaking in lively discussion, and knowing that others may have valid suggestions to offer. To the best of my knowledge, successful shows are not created in a vacuum."
>
> —**BETH BOHN**, Literary Agent, Owner of Bohn Management

Of course, it's your call to make. If you've created something deeply personal or have a particular celebrity attachment, you may decide not to entertain the exec's spitball input and either gently reiterate your show's concept or end the meeting. With *Launching Allee*, I had a brilliant creative mind at the heart of the show whose only real request was that we not be one more in a chain of hyper-manipulated reality series about celebrities, as innovation and experimentation was such an integral part of her core philosophy. We made up our minds early on to not compromise

9 Don't do this.

the integrity of what we'd set out to produce. But when you're pitching something that *isn't* a piece of your soul and collaboration comes a-calling, my general advice is to let it ride.

So the executive is sold on your show about the animal handlers, except now it's a game show for kids in which the animal handlers trot out different animals that families have to answer trivia questions about in order to win a vacation. Now what?

Well, the first thing that'll happen is a lot of legal stuff that your agent and/or entertainment attorney will have to hammer out for you. I cannot express how important it is that you not navigate your own deal-making, or how dangerous it is to proceed on a handshake or informal verbal agreement.

If you're a creator who's just pitched a production company to partner with in the name of gaining access and clout, each party's attorneys will have to establish who will own how much of the show, what happens in the event of a sale, your probable on-screen credit, and (most importantly) how long the producer/production company has to try to sell the show to a buyer. Often, these kinds of agreements are for less than six months, sometimes as limited as ninety days. Why put a time limit on such an arrangement? While they can always be extended by mutual agreement, you don't want your show tethered to a company that suddenly changes its mind and decides to stick your hard work in a drawer for all eternity, leaving you frustrated.

It also provides you with an escape hatch in the event that the production company you've partnered up with doesn't deliver. Same drawer, different scenario.

Did I mention that production company agreements don't usually come with a check? These alliances are about forming a partnership that will strengthen you and your show in the room with a network by proving that a viable, experienced company is standing ready to produce your show if they decide to say "Yes."

Let's say you've managed to pitch directly to a network without a production company on board. The network will likely either partner you with a production company who's successfully produced something for them in the past or recommend a handful of production companies for you to meet with and select from.

In the case of an unproven newbie, your agent or entertainment attorney will negotiate an agreement for you after which you'll most likely have virtually nothing to do with the show other than sit at home and watch your credit roll by every week. If you're a mid-career reality or other entertainment media professional, you're far more likely to successfully negotiate a role in production and remain involved. Be realistic in your expectations.

Remember that vision you had about wrapping your hands around the wheel of your new Mercedes? Trust me, that first sale isn't likely to land you in Malibu.[10] But what it will do is give you credibility as a creator that you can bring with you to the table next time. The career of a reality show creator isn't a sprint, it's a marathon.

---

10 I strongly suggest reading Donna Michelle Anderson's *The Show Starter Reality TV Made Simple System: Ten Steps to Creating and Pitching a Sellable Reality Show* for more on the realities of selling a first show.

Chapter Eight Exercises

CREATE A SHOW

Start with writing a simple logline that conveys the concept for your show. Share it with a few friends. Do they "get" the concept when they read your logline?

Develop a pitch. How would you sell the show if you only had one minute? How about three?

Move on to writing a three- to five-page treatment. Again, share with friends to see if the treatment adequately clarifies your concept and conveys what an episode would look like and where the show could go in subsequent seasons.

Finally, write a script for a one- to three-minute sizzle reel. One more time, share with some trusted friends to ensure that the sizzle clearly explains the concept.

Going to Market

So you've got your materials down and you're ready to pitch. Now . . . how do you get in the door?

Most major production companies don't consider unsolicited material, meaning that they don't want to review anything they haven't asked to see. It's a way to not only keep hundreds of amateur submissions from choking their resources, but also avoid nuisance lawsuits from people who blindly submit projects and then sue over tangential similarities in projects the company may put out down the line. Submitting through an agent or entertainment attorney is preferred, if not required.

Agents and Managers

If there's one thing traditional scripted content and reality shows have in common, it's the perennial question from newbies about whether or not an agent/manager is a necessary part of the equation.

When discussing representation for reality clients who primarily write and produce at an early- to mid-career level, all we need to discuss are agents. Agents are licensed by the state, while managers are not. Agents can seek out and procure work for their clients, while managers cannot. Managers primarily handle clients whose careers are already on track and are primarily charged with keeping them happy.

They also have the advantage of being able to both package *and* produce their clients' material, a trend that really picked up speed a decade or so ago, primarily on the side of traditionally scripted entertainment.

Be aware that a number of agencies have the word "Management" in their title. Without going too far down the rabbit hole of insanity in explaining it, just know that your agent could work at International Creative Management, or perhaps the Creative Artists Agency, both of which are referred to as "agencies."

Now that we've established that what you're probably looking for is an agent and not a manager, let's first discuss what an agent really does, versus what most people imagine they do.

As Chad Gervich describes in his book *How to Manage Your Agent*,[1] their function is fivefold:

- To find work
- To negotiate contracts, deals, and other agreements
- To gain information and access
- To be a creative guide or sounding board
- To offer legal and contractual guidance or protection

While I know a great many reality professionals who work without benefit of agency representation, they're usually folks who've been in the business for a stretch and have developed their networking game well enough to keep the ball rolling on their own. Whether working on other people's shows or out creating and pitching, they're gaining access by way of relationships formed over their careers.

If, however, you need access and some career guidance, you could probably benefit from representation — the catch there being that there aren't a lot of agencies gunning for fresh, unproven talent. This is another reason why I say that trying to break in as a show creator without spending some time in the reality trenches is a rough go.

Finding representation in reality/alternative from a cold start is hard, and to be frank, it's unlikely that you'll be signed anywhere until you're inside the business and working at a Story Producer level or above. Demonstrating a track record of earning money in the field goes a long way, as

---

1 *How to Manage Your Agent*, Chad Gervich, Focal Press, 2014. This is an essential read for those looking to understand and maximize their agent-client relationship.

agencies are not primarily in the business of philanthropy. They want to make money just as you do, but since they work on commission, developing talent from scratch is a costly proposition for them.

I managed to land representation in alternative by finding a fellow alumnus from film school who was working as an assistant to an agent at APA.[2] As I'd already been working in reality for a while, it was easy to show that they'd be able to make at least a little money by representing me. Eventually, I was kicked up the ladder to Beth Bohn, a Senior VP at the agency whom I followed to her new company some years later.

You can always go the route of writing an agency query letter and hoping to set up a meeting, but keep in mind that the way into many places is finding ways to interact with working professionals who might eventually refer you to their representation. Getting some work under your belt that will make you seem appealing to agencies doesn't hurt, either.

---

2 Agency for the Performing Arts.

CASE STUDY:
BETH BOHN, BETH BOHN MANAGEMENT

Beth Bohn is a former Senior VP at APA who now owns and operates Beth Bohn Management, where she represents television clients from all areas and disciplines including producers, writers, directors, and production companies.

The television business is one in which the relationships you cultivate are every bit as important as your ability to execute great content. On the rare occasions when I refer mid-career friends[3] to Beth (who doesn't take unsolicited material), I make sure that they've got a vision for their future and some existing connections to build on rather than simply wanting to work. Why? Because I know that as an agent, she's usually looking to work with people who have a desire to build and advance to the big leagues rather than just pick up a check here and there.

Says Beth, "The people who really throw themselves into the business are the people who will get ahead. I find people right out of college who are not serious about what they're doing, so they screw up and hurt their career."[4]

Just as important as finding representation after you've built up a few credits is this: It matters whom you sign with. It's not enough to find representation; you've got to find an agent who understands you and can help you to hone your game plan. What you don't want to get stuck with is an agent or agency that signs many clients, but can only devote time to their top earners and superstars. You might as well walk up to a stranger on the street and offer them 10% of your income for the next decade.

Beth advises, "Whatever size agency you sign with, you need to find someone who loves your work and gets your writing so they will be passionate and fight for you."[5]

---

3 Never unproven new talent.

4 *The Screenwriter's Guide to Agents and Managers* by John Scott Lewinski, Allworth Press, 2001.

5 Ibid.

> **CASE STUDY TAKEAWAY:**
> While agents and managers are important players in the life of a reality
> professional, it's important to find the right match, be able to present
> yourself as a viable client with experience under your belt and a fire to
> succeed, and have realistic expectations.

Your Networking Game

Yeah, I know. We've already covered networking in Chapter Seven. But
now that you're out there trying to sell a show instead of simply finding
your way in, we have more to discuss.

So you know that an agent or some sort of representation is important, but whether you're trying to sell a show or just yourself, your own
legwork is key — and this is true whether you have representation or not.

If you live in or near a major entertainment industry city, like Los
Angeles, New York, Chicago, or Atlanta, watch for events in your area
that are regularly attended by television professionals. Look for events
like NATPE[6] Pitchcon, or if your reality concept is better suited for the
Internet, Stream Market. Other organizations often put on seminars
and luncheons that draw professionals you can interact with and build
acquaintanceships.

While you may feel compelled to pitch on the spot when you meet
someone in the business, don't force your idea on them. Ask for advice
and permission to contact them down the line about your concept. Sometimes, this leads to an opportunity to meet formally somewhere later,
where you're not vying for their attention in a small crowd. Other times,
the exec might tell you who to call at their company, so you can make
your introduction to the correct party with a simple "My name is (blank)
and (exec) suggested I call you to discuss a reality series we talked about
at (event). When might be a good time for you?"

If you have an agent, let them make that call.

---

6 National Association of Television Program Executives.

I don't care what you've heard about non-disclosure agreements, but when a first-time creator wants to submit a show and tries to get a production company to sign one before they can hear the pitch, it's a major, unforgivable hack move. It signals that you don't trust the process or the company. Sure, you'll be asked to sign one when a company hires you to work on a project, but it doesn't go the other way.

When an agent sets a meeting for your work, there's a record of having set the meeting. You, of course, have already registered your work with the WGA at *http://WGA.org* and the copyright office at *http://copyright. gov*. You have nothing to worry about, and if your pitch suddenly becomes a project without you, you have legal recourse.[7]

So please, please, *please*, don't be the NDA weirdo.

---

7 Remember, though — these companies may already have ideas just like yours in development. Don't leap to the conclusion that your idea's been stolen if you see something similar from them down the line, especially if it's only tangentially similar.

Chapter Nine Exercises

REGISTERING YOUR CONCEPT

Visit *http://WGA.org* and *http://copyright.gov*. Familiarize yourself
with the process of registering your original concepts.

When reviewing the forms at *http://WGA.org* (after clicking on
"Register Your Script" on the lower right side of the home page), take
special note of your options on the registration pull-down menu. You
can select from concept, treatment, game show, pitch, or other options
suited to what you'd like to register.

WHAT'S SELLING?

Get an impression of what the market is after by reviewing a few
weeks' worth of notices in the trades like *www.Deadline.com*, *www.
TheWrap.com*, *www.Variety.com* and others.

Take note of the creators and their representation in the write-ups.
Get to know who the agencies and reps are who are negotiating those
sales. Learn the names of the power players at networks mentioned in
the articles.

Next, work on making yourself conversationally fluent about
what's going on in the marketplace. Discuss some recent reality sales
with a friend, and how those sales might lead you to believe that a
buyer who pulled the trigger on those shows might enjoy a show that
you have ready to pitch.

Understanding the Global Market

It's a big world out there, and yes, it needs ideas. Let's think outside your own national borders for a moment, no matter what they may be.

Why Sell Overseas?

While the United States and the UK remain top exporters of television formats and programming, they're certainly not the only game in town.[1] Getting a show on the air somewhere, *anywhere*, opens doors. Formats originating in Denmark, Israel, or Japan, for example, may be adapted dozens of times around the world.

Major reality and game shows like *Iron Chef*, *Rising Star*, and more have been adapted in multiple countries where local versions are produced in the same manner that *American Idol* has been resold the world over. *Rising Star* has been adapted in more than twenty-five countries so far . . . an unqualified smash hit. A show that fares well locally or whose unproduced "paper format" is sold in multiple markets abroad can quickly become a real cash cow.

---

1 And by town, I mean on Earth.

Case Study: Avi Armoza / Armoza Formats

While the entire nation of Israel may have fewer television sets in total than the residents of Los Angeles County alone, you'd never know it by the size of their global footprint as developers and distributors of formats. Three companies — Keshet, Dori Media, and Armoza Formats — dominate Israel's TV formats landscape.

Avi Armoza is the founder and CEO of format powerhouse Armoza Formats in Tel Aviv, which has been proving itself globally since 2005. Avi's empire is founded on exporting both new and existing formats to countries all over the world. In the United States, NBC's multiseason hit *I Can Do That*[2] is but one of the formats he represents, and he has placed game shows, comedies, dramas, reality-competition shows, and more in places like the BBC and Channel 4 in the UK, Germany's RTL, and TL1 in France.

Says Avi, "From a commercial point of view, we are a small country and our outlets are limited; the creativity that exists here is much more than the local market can absorb. This is why many Israelis are looking to the international market, because if you know how to make television [. . .] why don't you look at the world as your market?"[3]

As of this writing, here's a sample of Armoza's reach: In a short span of time, *I Can Do That* (developed with Chinese broadcaster JSBC) has been sold into Romania, France, Spain, Italy, Portugal, Germany, Norway, Bulgaria, Russia, the United States, and more. Countless other Armoza originals and co-productions, including *The Gran Plan* and *Couch Diaries,* continue to rack up other international co-productions as well.

CASE STUDY TAKEAWAY

Remember, it's a big world out there. Don't just think about the production companies and networks native to home. Tap into universal themes relatable to any viewer, anywhere, and the world's your oyster.

---

2 As of this printing, *I Can Do That* has been sold into more than fifteen countries.

3 Interview with Anna Carugati, *www.WorldScreen.com,* 9/13/2013.

Retaining Your IP Rights

"Intellectual property," defined as creative work to which ownership can be assigned by copyrights, trademarks, and other protections, is incredibly valuable. Applying IP rights to reality formats remains a legally complex endeavor, primarily because it's so hard to define and nail down the value of each component. This is because reality programs are analogous to traditionally scripted shows, but have additional elements not present in those scripted shows.

Where you sell your work determines the protections afforded to you as a creator/producer and what components of the show you own. It almost goes without saying that the single or shared rights to a format or any part thereof translates to money down the line when a show is sold into other territories.

Copyright may cover things like theme songs, scripts, and storyboards, while catchphrases and slogans may be registered for trademark. Technologies and gimmicks unique to a production (think about *Survivor*'s torches that are snuffed on elimination) may be covered by copyright, as might host copy.[4] When your project starts traveling the world, ensure that all your applicable rights are secure. Familiarize yourself with IP law in other countries when it comes time to negotiate, as it could be of tremendous benefit to you down the line. My two cents? Always, always, always consult a lawyer with experience in international IP rights.

---

4 "UK: Intellectual Property Rights in TV Show Formats," by Margaret Tofalides and Alastair Bleakely for Addleshaw Goddard LLP, 2001.

Chapter Ten Exercise

INTERNATIONAL FORMAT EXERCISE

It's been said that family content may travel best internationally, as it has what the industry refers to as four-quadrant appeal (male, female, under twenty-five, over twenty-five). Reality competition and game often fulfills this requirement.

Using the Internet, research a few reality/game formats that have been successful internationally but have not yet been adapted in your home country, then answer these questions:

- Does this show appeal to all four quadrants?
- Where would this show air in your home country?
- If the show is too unlike anything on the air at home, what would you change to make it more appealing to viewers in your country?
- What does the success of this show in its country of origin tell you about viewers there? Are their tastes that different than those at home?

CHAPTER ELEVEN

Parting Shots

Sometimes good advice doesn't fall into neat little chapters, which brings us here. I've asked fellow pros to share their own thoughts and stories on their careers in reality television.

Paula Aranda

Paula Aranda serves as Manager of Development and Production at VH1, where she's worked since 2009.

How did you find your way into reality television?
I started out in reality TV as an intern for VH1. I was always a huge fan of the shows, so I made it my mission to get a full-time job in the development department. Lucky for me, I got hired as an assistant and was able to move my way up over the years.

What kind of education do you find most useful for someone considering the exec path?
The most useful education is one that familiarizes you with as many reality shows, past and present, as possible. Watching TV is the best way to get a sense of what works.

What's the best point of entry for someone considering a career at network?
From my experience, starting as an assistant is one of the most direct paths. Unfortunately, you have to start from the

bottom, but being an assistant can also be extremely valuable — you have access to an executive and can learn from them without the pressure.

What would be the most significant piece of advice you'd pass on to someone considering a career in reality television?
Passion. If you are passionate about reality TV, a fan of reality, a viewer of reality TV, it will show.

What makes a great show for you?
A show that is real. It's easy to make a show where everything is laid out in advance and you just have to film specific scenes to tie it all together, but a more valuable show is where the cast can be themselves and isn't told what to do.

What's your most frequently given note — the one thing that you find important, but that you find yourself asking for again and again?
It's so important to let scenes breathe. Give comedy a chance to play out, or don't be afraid to sit in silence for a beat.

What's the biggest change in the business since you started?
So many shows have started to look and feel the same because the market is oversaturated. It's hard to find something that feels fresh.

What kind of shows do you wish there were more of?
I wish there were more shows that were real. Shows where you don't see the producer's hand telling the cast what to do.

To what do you attribute your longevity in the business of reality?
Loving what I do.

Brian Gibson

Brian Gibson has served as an Executive Producer of Top Gear, *Supervising Producer for* Supernanny, *and was the original Story Producer for* Dancing with the Stars *at the time of its ABC debut in 2005.*

What was your professional history prior to beginning your reality TV career?

I used to work as a development assistant for production companies, reading scripts and giving notes. Plus, answering phones, making copies, that kind of thing.

Did any of your skills from your pre-reality career carry over?

Not particularly. A development assistant needs to have a fundamental understanding of storytelling, and in particular, film storytelling, but I feel like I acquired that from a lifelong love and study of film, TV, and literature.

Do you agree that it is necessary to obscure the writing process for reality in order for audiences to invest in shows? Why?

Not at all. People don't really expect their entertainment to be real. Look at wrestling. People still love magic, don't they? Any form of entertainment requires suspension of disbelief, and being comfortable with illusion. The audience for these shows is smarter and more aware of how things are done than ever before. I think that fans enjoy an understanding of how their favorite shows are made, and in reality TV I think they enjoy knowing what is and isn't written, and why.

What's the most valuable piece of advice you could give to someone considering a career in reality television?

Take some pride in what you do. Even though you might have other career goals outside reality, work hard, don't wait for your ship to come in, it probably won't. Network, save up a little, be prepared to find a new job every four to six months.

—

Pam Malouf

Pam Malouf is an experienced Editor whose stellar credits span film and television projects from Star Wars *to* Dancing with the Stars, MacGyver *to* The Apprentice. *As you can imagine, she really knows her stuff.*

What kind of story staff makes a job wonderful/awful for you?

A lot of Story Producers say that they can't provide bites or a bite structure without seeing all the shot material. Yet as Editors, when we are confronted with twenty to eighty hours of material, it can become overwhelming and if we have a bite structure, even if it's a "wish list," then it gives us a direction and we can cut much faster and more efficiently. The bite structure is like the spine, and we can find and build the reality (body) around it. Sure, sometimes the reality is great and a clear story presents itself and then the bites (or spine) are requested and inserted into the body. Sometimes it's a bit of 50-50. Often, the story can go many different directions so at least a bite structure as a guide — preferably double the needed bites so we have options to use based on the material — then it's much easier and faster to craft the reality around the bite intentions. It's awful when, as an Editor, you're wading in hours and hours of material, with many different options of directions to go in or focus on and a Story Producer tells you they can't give you any bites unless they see everything! Come on, Story Producers — surely you know that Editors can manipulate and manufacture moments — so give us some kind of guidance in the form of bites.

What do you wish newly minted Story Producers knew about your process?

Often, as Editors we have pulled interesting moments, "selects," but we're not sure what to do with them or if they could have value. A Story Producer who knows what selects are (also referred to as "pulls") and can view these selects and understand that they are not in any particular order but instead are moments that can be rearranged and formulated into a story is helpful. A Story Producer who starts giving editing "notes" on selects is very annoying. Just tell us which ones you think have value, if you think we might have a story somewhere, what order could these go in? Listen to our bite suggestions.

How important is it for story to have a good "ear"?

With the proper bites, we can help you make a story out of nothing or anything.

It'd be nice if every story person knew what a "frankenbite" is and that not just anything will cut together. You need endings of sentences, consonants cut up better than soft vowels. In other words, be realistic when you hand us bites on paper.

Also transcriptions, logs, whatever you want to call them — often oversell content, so if something is critical to the story ask to see it right away so that if it doesn't work (camera is on the floor, shooting the wall or wiggling, making content unusable), we can go in another direction or down a different story path.

How do you handle "problem" story folks, those who you find difficult to work with or who ignore your needs as an Editor?

Problem story folks often are not focusing on the story. They are trying to talk you, as Editor, into cutting in something that they think is really funny but is a total non sequitur and has nothing to do with the story. Or if you cut in the piece they want they have no bites to tie it in or make it work and create a problem sequence.

Sometimes a Story Producer gets stuck on something they read in a transcript and even when you show them that the camera was on the wall they still insist on trying to work it in when it's impossible. They need to know when to move on and take a different approach, come at the story from another angle.

Or they hang out in your bay and go online and make noise (talking on the phone), park at your desk while they eat their lunch and talk to you about personal issues while you are trying to edit. This type of behavior in the edit bay is just a distraction and slows down the cutting process. Once you've told us what we need to know — get out! Tell us to call you when we are ready to show you something else, or ask us to call you as soon as we have more selects pulled, but don't just hang out.

Supervising Producer Dena Waxman consults with Story Producer Kanika Utley and Editor Stuart Archer. (photo courtesy of Dena Waxman)

CHAPTER TWELVE

Closing

Well, you've made it to the end of this second edition of *Reality TV.* [1]

As with the first edition, I am deeply grateful for the participation of my industry colleagues who candidly related their experiences and freely offered their advice, and to the many people whose research and other published writings helped make this book feel like more than one man's opinionated musing on his craft.

I hope that you will take to heart my advice about working your way up through reality television rather than showing up on its doorstep, kicking at the door with original shows. Coming up is half the fun, and the one thing you'll learn that way that no other route can provide is how to navigate the politics within certain companies and networks, how to make friends and find mentors, and how to develop that web of support that makes working in this business so much fun. [2]

As I said in the closing of the previous edition, at its best, reality TV inspires and educates, entertains and enlightens; at its worst, it provides us, at least, with some pretty compelling examples of how *not* to behave. In other words, it does exactly what books, movies, and other kinds of television have always done. The great sin is doing any

---

1 And here I am with neither coffee nor dessert at the ready.

2 Occasionally awful, but mostly fun. Even ice cream–testers have bad days.

of it without passion, inflicting dull storytelling on anywhere from a few thousand to tens of millions of viewers at a time.

Care about the work.

If you're sincerely interested in a career in reality, I wish you the best of luck, success, and happiness in the field . . . and don't forget to write![3]

---

3 Check out *www.realitytvbook.com*, where you'll find my "contact" page.

Glossary

Usually, any online or reference glossary of production terms is helpful in explaining the basics — but as terms can vary slightly in meaning as you shift from traditionally scripted programs to reality, here's one with the appropriate reality "spin" applied to select terms:

aerials: Shots filmed from an airplane, helicopter, balloon, etc., often used as B-roll when establishing a location. Watch almost any show set in Vegas or Miami for an idea of what great aerials should look like.

ambient sound: Sometimes referred to as "nat sound," short for "natural sound," ambient sound includes everything from traffic noise to background chatter in a restaurant.

ASCAP: American Society of Composers, Authors and Publishers. ASCAP collects licensing fees on behalf of its members whenever you use music in your show. See also BMI and SESAC.

aspect ratio: The dimensional ratio (width to height) of an image, 4:3 for conventional standard definition and 16:9 for HDTV.

assembly: A stringout that arranges source clips in a sequence similar to the order in which they'll appear in the final product, providing the starting point for your Editor.

Associate Producer: As credits vary in meaning from production to production in reality, an Associate Producer credit can be bestowed on almost anyone from a Story Assist to a member of your field crew to a particularly valuable Production Assistant.

audio mixer: The member of your field crew responsible for ensuring the quality of audio being recorded on location. The term also applies to the device the audio mixer uses in the field to direct audio to assigned tracks at manageable levels.

B-roll: Supplementary footage that helps you to better illustrate your story in montage or cutaway. B-roll includes everything from aerial shots of a location to shots of wringing hands in interviews to crowd shots not featuring your cast.

bin: Editing term describing a database that simplifies the organization of digitized material. In verb form, the action of organizing source material within bins: "Bin out that Las Vegas B-roll for me, would you, Adam?"

BMI: As with ASCAP, BMI (Broadcast Music Incorporated) is a company that licenses music and collects royalties.

boom: The microphone-on-a-pole you're always complaining about winding up in the shot in your source material, as in, "I can't believe the boom is completely ruining that take!"

burn-in: Information, usually time code, that appears in a window superimposed over a video image. Especially useful in the notes process, a time code burn-in helps your producers and network folks to pinpoint changes: "At 01:04:34, let's cut the reference to peanut butter sandwiches."

call sheet: A printed or digitally delivered list of cast and crew members detailing at what times and locations they're expected to appear on a given day. Call sheets should also include contact information for everyone involved as well as the production office.

call (or call time): The time you or another crewmember is due to be on set or at some specified location, as in, "I can't go out tonight, I have a 5:30 a.m. call in Long Beach."

clearance: Documented permission allowing use of an image or music.

clipping: An audio term describing instances where audio signal overwhelms equipment's recording limits, resulting in distortion or noise. You'll know it when you hear it.

credits: That list of everyone who worked on a show that runs at the top or end of each episode. Make sure they spell your name right!

cross-fade: When one audio or video source dissolves into another. More often referred to in the edit bays as a "dissolve" when relating to video.

cue: A music track used in your edit. For example: "Hey, Adam, can we replace the first cue in the restaurant scene?"

cutaway: A shot that we "cut away" to in a scene to add context to an interview or dominant action, sometimes used to compress time. Example: During an interview in which a cast member complains about another cast member always losing her keys, you can insert a cutaway of the cast member searching for her keys.

deal memo: The offer of employment and the terms of same memorialized in a document. See Appendix E to learn more about deal memos.

dissolve: A transition in which the first image loses intensity while the next gradually overtakes it. In reality TV, dissolves are most often used to illustrate a passage of time.

dub: A copy of a video or audio product. Nowadays, more often referred to as an "output" or a "DVD." Where once we said, "Let's dub a copy of this for the network," we now say, "Let's knock a DVD out to send over to the network," or "Can we get an output of this sent over to network?"

Dubber: The individual who copies video or audio product for circulation.

edit: To refine and rearrange source material into an acceptable end product.

edit bay: The room where editing takes place.

Editor: The person whose job function is to edit.

establishing shot: A shot used at the top of a scene to let you know where you are. Usually city shots, building exteriors, or signage.

Executive Producer (or EP): Typically the decision-making top banana to whom everyone reports. Usually, EPs don't oversee the technical end of production.

frankenbite: An interview or OTF statement cobbled together from fragments of other sentences to create the illusion of naturally occurring speech. I suggest that these be used judiciously (a bad one sounds lousy and blows the illusion of reality) and ethically.

genre: A categorization of a particular product as a result of theme or content. Reality shows are a genre, just as comedies and dramas are.

hot sheet: A brief summary of each day's shoot sent back from the field to keep Producers and story people not present in the field informed as to what's going on.

interview: Formal Q&A with a character that provides insight into events anticipated or recalled, often covering the details of a day to a few days of activity after the fact.

jump cut: An undesirable cut in which a slightly altered position or action by a performer on each side of the cut produces a jarring, rough effect rather than a smoother, relatively unnoticeable transition.

lavalier mic (or lav): A small microphone usually attached to clothing. Ideal for gathering audio unique to an individual in-scene, as opposed to boom coverage, which provides little to no ability to single out audio tracks for individuals in-scene.

log: A written transcript (varying in detail by production needs) of the content found in source footage. Camera logs are usually generated in the field and are very general in content; logs executed in post tend to be more detailed and provide a useful, timesaving tool as a searchable database for tracking down specific actions or dialogue. In verb form, the act of logging: "Log those August 9 tapes for me, Adam."

Logger: A person who creates logs in post, supporting the story department and Editors.

montage: A series of shots strung together either to establish a mood or location or evoke a sense of something being accomplished without going so far as to create a scene. You know the latter — Judy tries on ten dresses in fifteen seconds while her friend frowns at all but the last one.

nat sound / natural sound: see **ambient sound**

noise: Noticeable interference on source audio or action for action's sake (an illogical escalation of activity and tone in-scene) as in: "That fight is completely unmotivated and has nothing to do with our story; I think we're just cutting for noise."

Offline Editor: The Editor who works with story to refine the episode through the various stages leading up to the fine cut.

Online Editor: The Editor who finalizes a project into an airable master.

OTF: "On the fly" interview. These are usually done minutes or hours after action happens, and at their best should capture immediate reactions to an event.

paper cut / paper edit: A text version of your script, usually prepared for assembly by an Assistant Editor as a starting point for your Editor.

postproduction: The process that occurs after shooting and ending with the delivery of a complete, airable master.

preproduction: The period of preparation that precedes shooting, including funding the show, finalizing a budget, hiring cast and crew, and composing outlines and shot lists.

Producer: A crew member or exec who oversees some specialized aspect or aspects of a production.

production: The period of time during which content is shot.

release: Documented permission to use the image of an individual or a location. Unreleased persons in a reality program will have to be blurred or otherwise edited out of your show. Ever see a room full of cloudy, ghost-like, blurry faces on a reality show? They're the unreleased folks.

SAG-AFTRA: A union under whose auspices most on-camera reality talent is covered. Formed in 2012 by the merger of the Screen Actors Guild and the American Federation of Television and Radio Artists, its mission is to ensure proper working conditions and adequate compensation for performers.

set: Location where action is taped.

shot list: A sort of shopping list for your Field Producer that details the shots they plan to get on location.

source material: The original video and audio material you have to work from.

Story Assistant: A person who supports the Story Producers and Supervising Story Producers by finding bites, source material, and occasionally executing scenework.

story department: The sector of a production embodied by Story Assistants, Story Producers, and Supervising Story Producers.

Story Producer: A person who is responsible for working source material into a coherent end product in conjunction with an Editor.

stringout: A loose assembly of story material and selects created by members of the story department for further refinement into an end product by the Editor.

Supervising Story Producer: A person who oversees the story department and is usually responsible for setting the tone and overall arc of a season within the parameters set down by his or her superiors.

talent: Reality participants on-camera as well as hosts or narrators, even if the latter only "appear" in narrative voice over.

temp track / temporary track: Music that is likely to be replaced later in an edit due to clearance issues. You might not be able to clear that U2 song you like, but until you find something that feels similar, you Editor can work with it until a suitable replacement similar in feel is decided upon.

time code: Track on source tape / source material that allows you to refer to specific moments in action, as in: "Show me the fight at 01:12:36, Adam." From a technical standpoint, it's also useful when grouping action from multiple cameras in edit so that all angles can be synced to view simultaneously.

Transcriber: The person responsible for translating content from taped interviews and spoken material into a text document that can be searched more easily.

transcript: Word-by-word text versions of content, usually only executed for interviews and lengthier OTFs. These are either executed by your in-house Loggers and Transcribers or by a professional transcription company.

unscripted programming: Reality TV purportedly shot without any sort of script or outline in place. Wince every time you hear the phrase, for you now know better.

verité: Unobtrusive observational style less reliant on artfully composed shots, keeping the hand of production invisible.

WGA: Writers Guild of America, a collective bargaining labor union for writers across the spectrum of film, television, and even some radio. Divided into two organizations, the WGAE and WGAW, which represent writers on the east and west sides of the Mississippi River, respectively.

Writing Host Copy and Voice Over

Someone's got to write all that stuff your host/narrator says, and when it's you, you'd better know how to write concise, compelling stuff.

Keep It Simple

There are many rules when it comes to writing host/narrator copy, but the one that tops the list is: Keep it simple. A clever turn of phrase now and again is fun, but get too cute with the content and you're going to drive your host (and everyone else) nuts.

The "Talk" Test

It's also quite important to remember your host's voice. You're not writing an electronics manual, it's got to sound like something a person would say. Moreover, something *your host* would say.

Is your host a comedian? A helpful, genial craftsman? A brassy no-nonsense guy?

Know who you're writing for, and aim for their voice. There's a reason that person was hired to host your show — and you've got to write to their personality.

It also helps, in the bigger picture, to remember that all this brilliant prose of yours has to come out of someone's mouth. Write copy like this at your peril:

103002A03 11:41:02 – 11:41:35 Carpenter struggles to place a beam in place.	HOST: RICKY CANNOT PLACE THE HALF-TON BEAM IN PLACE BECAUSE THE BRACKETS ARE NOT ALIGNED PROPERLY. HE CANNOT MAKE IT WORK, BUT IT IS HIS OWN FAULT. IT LOOKS LIKE THE FOREMAN WILL HAVE TO FIRE HIM.
103002A03 11:43:22 – 11:43:40 Foreman yells at Ricky.	10302A03 11:43:22 Foreman: "You're fired. Pack it up. You're off the job."

Say that content out loud. It sounds positively ludicrous. Nobody talks like that except robots.

Now give *this* copy the "talk" test:

103002A03 11:41:02 – 11:41:35 Carpenter struggles to place a beam in place.	HOST: RICKY'S NEW TO THE JOB, AND IT SHOWS. HE TRIES TO WRIG-GLE THE HALF-TON BEAM INTO PLACE, BUT THE BRACKETS ARE COMPLETELY MISALIGNED. IT'S JUST THE SCREW-UP FOREMAN PAUL NEEDS AS AN EXCUSE TO DROP THE HAMMER ON HIS INEXPERIENCED NEW HIRE.
103002A03 11:43:22 – 11:43:40 Foreman yells at Ricky.	10302A03 11:43:22 Foreman: "You're fired. Pack it up. You're off the job."

Much better!

A final thought: Should you find yourself writing copy for multiple hosts working together, remember that it's easier to assign blocks of declarative statements to each rather than attempting to write complex movie-like dialogue exchanges between them. They're often fed a line or two at a time on-set, and it makes the shoot go easier when they can just ad-lib a lot of "That's right, Paul" or "You guessed it, Carol" statements between them.

Things It's Not Your Job to Worry About (But That You Should Sweat Anyway)

A good Story Producer is always aware of what's coming back from the field and the problems it may present down the line. Whether you get the chance to chime in in the field or have to sort your issues out in post, there are a few specific things to watch out for that'll make life easier for you, your Editor, and your employers down the line.

Rights and Clearances / Releases

You'd be surprised at how much amazing content gets trashed or how many problems arise in postproduction because someone in the field forgot to get someone to sign a release form or thought that a cool B-roll shot of the "Hollywood" sign was fair game.

Ultimately, it'll come down to your Producer and production company's decision on how much risk they're willing to take. Lawsuits do get filed once in a while.

While your Field Producer or a Production Assistant in the field should be furiously working to maintain materials for a clearance binder that can be referred to later, sometimes things go awry in the heat of production and things get missed. Whether you're on location or just reviewing materials in post that you'd like to include in the show, here are some of the top clearance issues that can pose problems for you down the line.

Art

Whether you're shooting in a restaurant, an office, or someone's private home, keep an eye on what's on the walls. If your subject, for example, owns a large painting that hangs over the sofa, that prominently featured artwork must be cleared for use by the artist, artist's estate, or publisher. Ownership of the artwork is irrelevant . . . a buyer/collector can't just sign away the image.

Even if you're dealing with a mass-produced piece, you should be sure someone takes note of the artist and/or publisher in order to clear a work down the line. Failure to do so may force you to blur the image in post, which nearly always looks awful.

Cast Members

All cast members and persons they interact with on camera must sign a release.

Extras/Background

Any individual who's immediately identifiable in a shot they're walking through should be asked sign a release. If you're reviewing footage and there's no release for the guy at the table behind your cast who can't keep himself from staring over at the camera every few minutes, you'll probably wind up blurring his face in post.

Releases must be completely filled out and include, when possible, a photograph. If no photograph is obtained, a detailed description of the person written on the release may suffice (as in, "older man in red shirt, glasses, black baseball cap"). Where this is not possible, an area release should be posted to all entrances to the venue, stating that anyone entering the area grants permission for their image to be used.

HINs

Hull identification numbers (or HINs) are the sequences of numbers found on the sides of boats. Since they're used the same way as a license plate, you should consider having them blurred in post. Also be on the lookout for identification numbers appearing on sails.

Landmarks

While one might assume that certain landmarks are public domain, a number of them are protected by copyright or trademark. A couple of good examples are the Beverly Hills logo shield and, believe it or not, the famous "Hollywood" sign.[1]

License Plates

Fully legible license plates on automobiles should always be blurred in postproduction.

Logos

If your producers have done their jobs, you should never see a cast member in an obviously logoed shirt, cap, or jacket.

Logos are a gray area, as some brands are more protective of their use on-camera than others. One popular brand of men's shirts couldn't care less if you see the critter embroidered on the front, while others take great exception to seeing their duds on television. Sometimes all it takes to conceal one is a well-placed bit of colored tape; other times you'll have to blur them slightly in edit.

Sports team logos, unless cleared by prior arrangement, are absolutely no-go under any circumstances. Blur or avoid them.

Luxury car brands are also a big deal, so the next time you'd like to set up your wealthy character by showing off her car collection, think twice. You shouldn't have a problem if you've got a room full of vehicles or B-roll of a sports car rolling down the street with an unidentifiable driver as long as you remember to blur the license plates in post.

Minors

If you have a cast member with children at home, the parent or guardian will have to sign a release on the child's behalf. In many cases, both parents may be required to sign off on a minor, even if the couple has separated or divorced.

---

1 No kidding! Permission to use the "Hollywood" sign must be obtained from a company called Global Icons.

Personal Life Land Mines

Let's say one of your subjects is the ex-wife of a rock and roll legend who cheated on her in the most extravagantly public way possible. There are photos on the Internet, the next girlfriend (who got the same treatment) has sold her story to the tabloids, and the rocker in question is still being photographed with different long-legged beauties day after day after day. Can your subject say he cheated on her? Probably not.

As ludicrous as this sounds, lots of folks with lots of money to throw around love to go after shows for defamation. Talk with your production company's legal advisors or ensure that EP's sign off on accusations of infidelity, drug use, or anything else someone might take offense to having discussed. Fighting lawsuits costs money, whether the person who's coming after you is right or wrong, so why invite trouble?

One way around this, in some cases and depending on how risk-averse your employers are, is to ensure that the word "allegedly" finds its way into accusations made in interviews. There's a big difference between someone saying that some musician "is a drug addict" versus "is *allegedly* a drug addict." Two or three allegations by outside media sources supporting claims of "alleged" behavior can set your bosses' minds at ease.

Phone Numbers

Phone numbers featured in advertising, store windows, billboards, and so on may need to be blurred in postproduction.

Wide Area Releases

Whether you're shooting in a hair salon with strangers coming and going all day or at an event like a concert with hundreds or thousands of people in attendance, getting a wide area release is critical. These are posted on signs at all entrances to a venue warning people who enter that by doing so, their image and likeness may be recorded for broadcast. Your field team needs to not only post these signs, but also ensure that they get a shot of the sign at the location and in context (meaning that the sign and its location are both identifiable in the shot). Without this, the shots gathered at the event or location will likely have to be altered to blur the faces of folks seen therein, or worse yet, cost you use of the scene.

Product Integration / Product Placement / Tradeouts

No matter what stage of production you're brought in at, be sure to speak with your Supervising Producer about any existing commitments regarding product integration, product placement, or tradeouts. All three involve making sure products and services are somehow visible in conjunction with your storytelling, and will affect the decisions you make in selecting content.

With "product placement," you'll be required to incorporate plenty of recognizable logos but seldom (if ever) hear the product mentioned by name. Think of the Coca-Cola cups along the judges' table on *American Idol*. They have nothing to do with anything that's going on around them. No one's mentioning soft drinks, let alone their brand. Product placement simply puts brand-name items in view of the audience.

Moving on to "product integration," you may remember my earlier mention of the *Seventh Heaven* scripted storyline wherein the characters talked about Oreo cookies incessantly. The idea is to hear the name of the product in a way that can be perceived as organic to action.

Your cast may have to "hurry up and get in the Lexus" to get to their next destination, or simply figure out how "life is like a box of Junior Mints." Your show may go even further by creating challenges around specific products, as with a challenge featured on NBC's *The Apprentice* in which participants had to create their own specialty pizza for Domino's. The winning "American Classic Cheeseburger Pizza" was subsequently marketed by the company nationwide, capitalizing on the promotion the newly conceived product gained on the show.

Not all advertising is paid for. Sometimes, companies and services flat-out donate product in exchange for a little screen time in a process known as "tradeouts." When you see a room full of Dell computers or multiple characters checking messages on their sexy, ultra-high-end Sprint mobile phones in an extreme close-up with the logo visible, it's possible that the products could have been provided to the show as tradeouts. No money (or very little money) has changed hands in exchange for featuring the products.

Product placement and integration aren't always screamingly obvious, so asking for information about what's required to appear on screen is critical. If there are deals in place, a tradeout sheet may be available. This document will tell you what products have deals with the show, and what the conditions of those deals are.

Yours may look something like this:

Chewing Gum X
(Paid tradeout: $5000 plus chewing gum for cast/crew)
Requirements: Gum must be mentioned by name by a major character twice this season.

Auto Maker Y
(All cast and crew vehicles)
Requirements: Automobiles supplied must remain onscreen for a minimum of thirty seconds per episode with at least one brand-name mention or clearly featured logo.

Cell phone Company Z
(All cast mobile phones and service)
Requirements: Placement with logo visible in at least three episodes for minimum of three seconds.

Understanding Deal Memos

Once you're hired on a reality program, you'll be asked to sign an agreement called a "deal memo." If you work through an agency or an entertainment attorney, don't just reflexively sign the document and turn it in, as you'll want to have them look it over. If you're going it alone, there are a few things to look out for.

First, let's get a look at your deal memo:

DEAL MEMO

DATE: June 1, 2016
EMPLOYEE: Joe Blow

BIG REALITY COMPANY PRODUCTIONS, INC.
1322 Big Reality Company Drive
North Hollywood, CA 91601
818-555-1212
Re: Big Deal Reality Show Season 12

Dear Joe:
This is to set forth the terms and conditions of the agreement between you and Big
Reality Company Productions, Inc. ("Big Reality") regarding your position as "Story
Producer" (the "Position").

1.   Big Reality Company hereby engages you, subject to satisfactory performance, as a
"Story Producer." Your employment will commence on or about Monday, June 6, 2016 and
continue thereafter on a week-to-week, at-will basis until further notice. You will render
your services in the above-referenced capacity as assigned by Big Reality and under Big
Reality's direction and control.

2.   You will be paid $2,200 per calendar week (this includes the 10% agency Fee) of
employment in accordance with Big Reality's normal payroll practices. The default rule
of state income tax withholding is to withhold income tax for the state in which services
are performed (i.e., if you are traveling and working in a state other than California, taxes
may also be withheld for that state). This rate is not pay-or-play and employment is on an
at-will basis with Big Reality.

3.   The provisions of this letter and the attached Riders (A, B, C and D) shall constitute
the complete agreement between you and Big Reality concerning your position as "Story
Producer."

4.   A per diem will be paid for shoot days only while employed on location if applicable.

5.   Subject to Big Reality Company's discretion and approval, you shall receive an
"onscreen" credit as "Story Producer."

If this letter correctly sets forth our agreement, indicate your acceptance by signing both
copies of this letter, returning all copies to me.

With kind regards,
Big Reality Productions, Inc.

_____   _____
Fred Big (for Big Reality Productions, Inc)   Date

_____   _____
Joe Blow   Date

Seems pretty direct, doesn't it?

You've got a start date, the amount you'll be paid, and the credit you should receive outlined. Take a closer look, though, and see what you've really signed up for. You'll see many of these provisions time and time again, and they're always engineered to protect the company's interests, not yours.

First of all, take a peek at Sections 1 and 2 of your deal memo. Notice that phrase "at will"? That means that if you're no longer needed at any point, it doesn't matter if you were told you'd be on board for ten weeks or twenty, they can cut you loose at any time. Most companies are fairly inflexible on this, and while it seems frightening in contrast to traditional jobs that may offer two weeks' notice or severance, it's pretty much standard. The phrase pay-or-play refers to being paid whether or not your services are required and the show is in production or on hiatus. If your show goes down for a week for any reason, you may be sitting at home and not being paid.

In Section 2, you're offered $2200/wk, which is inclusive of your agency's 10%. That means your agency will be getting $220 per week from your gross, not in additional monies from the employer, Big Reality.

Section 3 refers to a series of riders that are not attached to the deal memo. How can you be expected to abide by terms you've never seen? Don't sign anything until you've seen everything. I'll tell you why in just a bit.

Section 4 states that you will be paid a "per diem" (an amount intended to cover your basic expenses) only while shooting on location. I wouldn't raise a fuss about it, but I'd ask whoever's doing your deal what the standard per diem is and whether it's paid in advance or at the completion of the shoot as a reimbursement. The amount is important . . . what if the per diem is $40/day and your location is a remote luxury resort where the cheapest thing on the hotel menu is a $23 omelet? You'll be eating once a day or going into your own pocket.

In Section 5, you'll be given a Story Producer credit at the sole discretion of the production company. While the possibility is remote, this may mean that your name may not appear in the end credits if your employment is terminated, if another Story Producer is brought in to rewrite your work, or if the network decides they want a shorter credit roll. I recently saw a show on National Geographic that referred viewers to their website to view production credits.

In Section 6, you're asked to sign both copies of the deal memo and return them to the company. Before you do that, you should probably make yourself a copy of the document for posterity, just as I'd always advise you to do with time cards.

While deal memos can be tricky business, it's wise to pick your battles and not appear to be too upset with anything you'd prefer to discuss or alter. I very seldom strike out and initial anything in a deal memo . . . but there is one thing I always add or review and revise: cross-indemnification provisions.

I know. You were enjoying the book up until I went all lawyer-ish on you. Sorry, but you should know how to protect yourself out there.

Aside from never signing a death or dismemberment waiver (which should be obvious), signing off blindly on indemnification clauses in a non-disclosure agreement is about the craziest thing you can do.

The Non-Disclosure Agreement and Cross-Indemnification

Here's a pretty dense bit of legalese that can get you in real trouble. Non-disclosure agreements protect the company in the event that one of their employees jumps online and blabs the dramatic end of the series to a social networking site or to the media. The show is devalued, meaning viewership may suffer and ad revenue may be lost. This only makes sense, but the amounts specified in non-disclosure agreements can be staggering. Two million dollars. Five million dollars. They're primarily in place to scare the pants off of you, and while they're rarely enforced, I don't suggest pressing your luck.

If phrasing in the document or any riders aims to put you on the hook for damages in the event that the show suffers some sort of financial hit as a result of your action or asks you to hold the producers harmless for any issues, I highly recommend writing in the phrase, "Agreed under condition of cross-indemnification" with your initials following next to the offending provision. In other words, you'll hold them harmless if they'll return the favor.

Remember, my advice here is no substitute for consulting a lawyer or your agent. These are merely notes from my own experience.

About the Author

TROY DEVOLLD'S TELEVISION CAREER started in 1990 when he was hired to write for a local Tampa television program called *Billy's Bogus B Movies*. He's been working in the reality television world since landing his first L.A. gig on MTV's *Fear* in August of 2000, eventually racking up credits on shows like *The Bachelor, Basketball Wives, Dancing with the Stars, Hollywood Game Night, The Osbournes, The Surreal Life*, and more. Along the way, Troy also shared an Emmy nomination with the production team of Style Network's *Split Ends* in 2009.

Photo by Patricia Harrison

Since the publication of *Reality TV: An Insider's Guide to TV's Hottest Market* in 2011, DeVolld has appeared on programs like *Today, Showbiz Tonight* and *AXS Live* as well as in the pages of *Time, Newsweek, Entertainment Weekly, A.V. Club, Emmy*, and more. He has lectured across the United States and abroad in conjunction with both the TV Writers Summit and StoryExpo, and has appeared on multiple panels in conjunction with the University Film and Video Association.

DeVolld is a graduate of Full Sail University, which honored him as the ninth inductee into its Hall of Fame in June of 2010. He is a member of the Academy of Television Arts and Sciences, where he has previously served as a mentor in conjunction with its College Television Awards, and also maintains membership in the Caucus for Producers, Writers & Directors. In addition to this book, he has also published the bestselling e-book *And Another Thing*, which explores the television notes process.

Troy lives on the outskirts of Los Angeles in beautiful Sunland, California. You can reach him at realitytvtroy@gmail.com or check out his blog at *www.realitytvbook.com*.

He is available on a limited basis for paid consultation and lecture events.

Despite this handsome write-up, he'd like you to know that none of this matters in the eyes of his do-nothing cat, Zoe.

THE MYTH OF MWP

In a dark time, a light bringer came along, leading the curious and the frustrated to clarity and empowerment. It took the well-guarded secrets out of the hands of the few and made them available to all. It spread a spirit of openness and creative freedom, and built a storehouse of knowledge dedicated to the betterment of the arts.

The essence of the Michael Wiese Productions (MWP) is empowering people who have the burning desire to express themselves creatively. We help them realize their dreams by putting the tools in their hands. We demystify the sometimes secretive worlds of screenwriting, directing, acting, producing, film financing, and other media crafts.

By doing so, we hope to bring forth a realization of 'conscious media' which we define as being positively charged, emphasizing hope and affirming positive values like trust, cooperation, self-empowerment, freedom, and love. Grounded in the deep roots of myth, it aims to be healing both for those who make the art and those who encounter it. It hopes to be transformative for people, opening doors to new possibilities and pulling back veils to reveal hidden worlds.

MWP has built a storehouse of knowledge unequaled in the world, for no other publisher has so many titles on the media arts. Please visit www.mwp.com where you will find many free resources and a 25% discount on our books. Sign up and become part of the wider creative community!

Onward and upward,

Michael Wiese
Publisher/Filmmaker